I

Copyright © 2012 Andy Leeks
All Rights Reserved

Dedicated to Emma and Charlotte.

Table of Contents

Wednesday 19th September 2012

Friday 21st September 2012

Monday 24th September 2012

Tuesday 25th September 2012

Wednesday 26th September 2012

Friday 28th September 2012

Monday 1st October 2012

Tuesday 2nd October 2012

Wednesday 3rd October 2012

Friday 5th October 2012

Monday 8th October 2012

Tuesday 9th October 2012

Wednesday 10th October 2012

Friday 12th October 2012

Monday 15th October 2012

Tuesday 16th October 2012

Wednesday 17th October 2012

Friday 19th October 2012

Monday 22nd October 2012

Tuesday 23rd October 2012

Wednesday 24th October 2012

Tuesday 30th October 2012

Wednesday 31st October 2012

Friday 2nd November 2012

Monday 5th November 2012

Tuesday 6th November 2012

Wednesday 7th November 2012

Tuesday 13th November 2012

Wednesday 14th November 2012

Friday 16th November 2012

Tuesday 20th November 2012

Wednesday 21st November 2012

Friday 23rd November 2012

Tuesday 27th November 2012

Wednesday 28th November 2012

Friday 30th November 2012

Monday 3rd December 2012

Tuesday 4th December 2012

Wednesday 5th December 2012

Friday 7th December 2012

Monday 10th December 2012

Tuesday 11th December 2012

Special Thanks

Foreword

As Andy greets me to discuss this 'book', he follows my opening pleasantry with the phrase "I'm absolutely knackered".

Given that the 'inspiration' for this tree waster was a Facebook row where he suggested people who sleep on trains are wasting their lives, there is more than a whiff of self righteousness in my nostrils.

Andy and I go back almost a decade, during which one of us has forged a career as a respectable mortgage broker, (with very reasonable rates by the way), and the other has become a sour-faced cretin, desperate to win a petty Facebook argument.

To my mind this is a pointless book - as ill conceived as his lifelong dedication to Watford football club.

So it's your call - you can inflate his ego and endure this nonsense, or you can just put it back in the bargain bin where you found it.

Whether you read on or not is up to you; just don't say I didn't warn you.

Dean Mason

Wednesday 19th September 2012

The reason I'm writing this now is something I wrote yesterday, on Facebook. I was on the 07:51 train into London and everyone around me was asleep.

I posted a status.

"Maybe I'm in the minority here, but it really annoys me when commuters sleep on trains, especially so on the morning leg. They have just had a whole night's sleep! You can get so much done on your commute, it's criminal to sleep through it"

Apparently I was wrong to assume people had enjoyed a whole night's sleep and there were doubtless many factors contributing to why they were sleeping. Many things could be responsible for their tiredness, such as work stresses or restless children.

I honestly didn't doubt for one second that these people had busy lives and that for them sleep was often at a premium; I was just making the point that using the commute to sleep was a waste of potentially valuable time. I then decided to list all of the things that could be done during their nap time. "You could pay some bills, research a recipe, get in touch with an old friend, catch up on the news, do some online shopping, enter a competition or even do some creative writing" I asserted.

By the time I had got to the last two, I had run out of ideas and my brain was pretty much running on empty. It is for this reason and this reason only that I then followed it up with the perhaps foolhardy promise: ".....In fact, I'll prove how much time you are wasting by sleeping - I am going to write something on every commute for a year!"

And just like that, this book was born. A challenge laid down to myself - to prove to all of those narcoleptic commuters just what could be done in those lost sleepy hours.

Exactly what I will write over the next year is as much a mystery to me as it is to you, but that is what makes it truly exciting. I have always loved a challenge, but I think this is the first time I have ever actually set one for myself. There is usually a friend involved and almost always alcohol to blame and/or a woman to impress. This time there is no alcohol, no woman to impress and there are certainly no friends involved.

Some days I imagine you will get some news, some days maybe a little story or anecdote, but almost every other day I expect you'll get me moaning about the fat bastard in the seat opposite, listening to his rubbish music, with a Tesco carrier bag between his feet, a can of Stella in his hand and an almost certain tragic early death ahead of him.

I kid you not - he has thundered through four cans of Stella in the time it has taken me to write this first entry! That's four cans in the time it has taken to get from London Cannon Street to Tonbridge. Four cans in 45 miles. That's a can every 11.25 miles. I hope this guy never travels long distance, it just might kill him. What if he tried to keep his can to mile ratio up on his holiday this year? Benidorm is 895 miles away, so that would be just short of 80 cans. Looking at him, I think he could give it a bloody good go.

My stop is approaching so I'll just go over the rules once again. I promise that this book will be written solely on my commute to and from work. That means that if I am not commuting, I am not writing.

There will be gaps where I am either ill, working from home or on holiday. Every day that I commute, I promise to add a chapter to this book. I'm adamant I won't spend my workdays, evenings or weekends writing. I have a job to do and a family to keep happy.

The whole point of this book is to show what can be done while commuting, and hopefully to prove once and for all that sleeping on trains really is a complete waste of time.

Friday 21st September 2012

The new school term was recently upon us, and the few weeks over the summer where the train was devoid of hormonal offspring was a pleasant and enjoyable time for me. That said, in some ways it's nice to have them back. They're so fresh-faced and innocent and their worries seem so trivial.

I've spent the last couple of days dealing with my inner demons, determined not to put the heating on until October the 1st. "Just another few days" I tell myself as I hop about, shivering in the early morning darkness. School children, however, have worries of a different kind. "I'm not sure if Olivia is talking to me, she didn't text me back after PE!" "Jack was on Facebook last night and he ignored my live chat request!" Depressing really, when you consider that school-children's worries and woes these days seem to revolve around social issues and very rarely actually involve school itself.

It was refreshing then this morning when I heard three girls debating which was their favourite day. "I like Mondays because we have double Maths, followed by P.E and R.S" said one "I like Wednesdays as we have Double

French, followed by History and Art" followed the other. It was easy to see that these girls were new to the school and therefore the timetable. They had the telltale signs – they had the clean blazers, the new bags, the shiny shoes and smiles on their faces. It probably won't be long before they are discussing their least favourite day and then I suppose it's a gradual slide towards the inevitable question, "Is Olivia talking to me?"

It would be nice if commuters talked about their days in the same way. "Tuesday's my worst day – it starts with a morning commute where I contemplate suicide, followed by small talk with the world's most boring receptionist, and finished off by a meeting with a room-full of arrogant arse-holes."

The great thing about school, and what children truly don't realise and unfortunately won't realise until it's too late, is that it is a lot of fun. It's a lot of fun because it offers a lot of variety. I remember one particular day at school where I had eight single lessons. Most days we had four double periods or a mixture of double and singles, but Wednesday was fun because we had eight different lessons. I can't remember exactly what we had on Wednesdays, but it was something like Maths, followed by English, followed by Geography, followed by P.E, followed by Science, followed by Art, followed by I.T, followed by French. Ok, it was a terrible way to end the day, but where else were we going to learn some foreign swear words? (And Miss Kleine was possibly the best looking teacher that I ever encountered.)

Just think though – what if we could incorporate that kind of variety into our working lives today? How great would it be to do a spot of Accounting, followed by Building, followed by Catering, followed by Bus Driving? Maybe that's the solution. No one would leave their job through boredom and it would be difficult to get the sack. Agreed, there would be a few things to iron out on the admin and logistical side, but I honestly think it could work.

Monday 24th September 2012

We had a birthday in the household this weekend as my wife turned 35, or as she likes to call it, her 30th birthday, plus 5. She is adamant she remains in her early to mid-thirties and will only cross over to her mid-thirties when she turns 36. At 37 and 38 she will still be in her mid-thirties, and finally at 39 she will then, and only then, and for one year only, be in her late thirties. We have not discussed what she will be when she turns 40, maybe she will be in her really late thirties or maybe she will be 30 plus 10.

Birthdays are strange things. Growing up, we never made a huge thing of birthdays. I can't really remember any parties being thrown and I distinctly remember the first time presents were replaced by vouchers and money. Birthdays are, after all, a lot of effort. If we're being honest, a birthday is simply a celebration of the day you were born. A day that is then celebrated year after year after year until you die. Here's the hard truth, people – enjoy your birthdays when you are young, because by the time you turn 21, you will have had all of the birthday excitement that you are ever going to get.

Year 22 and upwards will be a succession of disappointment for you and stress for your loved ones as you try and fail to drop hints about what you like and they in turn try and fail to spot interests and hobbies which never existed in the first place.

"I got you this because you mentioned once, when drunk, six years ago, that you'd like to try drawing with charcoal!"

"Thanks," you say as you try to decide whether it would be better off in the shed or the spare room, eventually deciding on the shed as that's where the other flammable items are kept.

I think it's right to have a big party when you're 21. You are celebrating finally becoming an adult. Sure, turning 18 gives you the right to poison your body with cigarettes and alcohol, but turning 21 gives you the maturity to deal with it. For instance, when you're 18, you'll go out and get irresponsibly drunk, mixing drinks, talking to strangers in kebab shops and throwing up over the dog. When you're 21 you will still go out and get irresponsibly drunk, mixing drinks, talking to strangers in kebab shops and throwing up over the dog, but you'll take a glass of water to bed.

What I suggest is to keep the 18th and 21st birthday parties, but introduce a new major celebration – the 22nd birthday party. This is where you gather all of your friends and family, (the advantage of this being that at 22 you still have plenty of both,) and you have one big final party which represents all of the birthdays that you will ever have in your lifetime. It's brilliant, because you can go through all of the emotions as you drunkenly celebrate your last ever birthday party.

You'll be sober at the start of the party and that will represent your sensible years, where people buy you a special pen for work, or a desk toy, or a new wallet. You'd then have a few drinks and be merry; this would represent your early twenties, with all of the hope and wonder, your life still ahead of you, a career to forge and a relationship to nurture. After a few more you might get a bit silly; this would represent the time that you decide to have a career change and go from being a solicitor to a bus driver, or when you decide to leave your wife for the boss's daughter.

After a drink or two more you will become emotional. This represents the time, approximately two years later, when you're driving that bus or having an argument with your new lover, when you sit down and think "What have I done with my life?" Eventually, at the end of the party, you'll be unconscious on the floor in a pool of your own sick and I don't need to tell you the years which this represents.

So there we have it. No more awkward gatherings, no more tedious meals out, no more surprise parties and no more birthday stress. If none of that is reason enough to introduce the 22nd birthday party, just think of the savings you'd make on candles.

Tuesday 25th September 2012

We have a two and a half year-old daughter and when she was about two and a half days old, we decided we needed to get a baby monitor. Ever the gadget man, and to my wife's initial horror, I walked in with a bit of kit that wouldn't have looked out of place in a police command centre.

It was a video baby monitor, but not just any old video baby monitor. It had a remotely controllable camera that allowed you to see any part of the room, and it had night-vision. The sort of night-vision that they use in those ghost-hunting programmes. Everything can be seen clearly in ghostly whites and greys and eyes show up as a weird kind of black.

To my surprise my wife grew to love it. She loved that she could not only hear what was going on, she could see it with her own eyes, without having to go into the room and turn on lights and disturb the baby. Suddenly, if there was a bump or a rustle, a quick check on the video monitor was all that was needed to see that the baby was safe and well. The only problem with this fancy bit of kit, however, is that we are now reliant on it.

A few weeks ago, one of the leads which charge the parent unit decided to die. It meant that we had to use the lead to the camera unit to charge the baby unit when it wasn't in use. Not ideal. In fact it was a complete pain in the arse. We checked online and there was no way of replacing the lead, and the product was no longer under warranty, but instead of buying a new monitor we carried on. We did so for two main reasons. Firstly, video monitors are relatively expensive, and secondly, we could not bring ourselves to buy an ordinary sound-only monitor – we had seen the other side. So our ridiculous routine went like this.

We'd wake up, unplug the camera unit and plug in the parent unit. For her afternoon sleep, we then had to unplug the parent unit and plug in the camera, now relying on the internal battery. When the baby woke up we unplugged the camera and plug in the parent unit. For the night-time sleep we'd have to unplug the parent unit and plug in the camera, once again relying on the internal battery. The problem was, however, that the internal battery only lasted six hours a best, so an hour before we went to bed, we unplugged the camera, plugged in the parent unit, opened baby's door and turned down the

TV after an hour. That gave us just enough charge to see us through until morning and then the whole thing would start again. What I didn't mention is that as we always had to rely on the internal battery and the battery life was so poor, we had to conserve energy by putting it on power-save mode, which meant that it was being used as a sound-only monitor for 99% of the time! We would often hear a noise, look at the battery indicator and weigh up whether it was worth taking a look.

Eventually we decided we needed to invest in a new monitor and of course, it had to be a video one. To my delight I found a monitor that had been reduced and instead of £150 it was being sold for £75. It was a reputable name and it was a reputable high street shop, so I purchased it without hesitation. (I have tried very hard to protect the shop that sold it to me, so I will not name it in any way and I hope I can tell my story without you being able to correctly identify the shop.)

To cut a long story short we got it home, tore off the protective packaging and set it up, and it was absolutely rubbish. It just didn't offer any sort of peace of mind because the video function was useless. It effectively provided us with a rectangle of grey. Fantastic if you like the colour grey and even better if your favourite shape is the rectangle, but in terms of providing us with a reassuring picture of our baby, it was absolutely pointless.

The next morning, I packed up all of the parts and put them neatly into the box that they came in. I then put the box in the blue bag that it came in and made sure I had the receipt stating my collection point. I got back to the shop, flicked through the catalogue, chose a replacement model (that was nearly double the price,) filled in the seven digit code with my little blue pen and then strode up to the customer services desk.

"I'd like to return this please." I said.
"Sure sir, what is wrong with it?" he asked.
"It's rubbish; this is the first time I have used this brand of monitor and it is not as good as our last one, it doesn't provide us with any sort of security – the picture is very poor." I said.
"No problem sir!" he said.

He then proceeded to check the returned item and asked where the protective packaging was. I explained that if he was talking about the small plastic bags that were sealed around the screen and camera, they were in the bin.

"Why is that?" he asked.

"Because they were torn" I said.

"In order to return an unwanted item sir, it needs to be returned in the same condition it was bought in…" he said.

"I understand that," I said, "but in order to open the item I needed to take it out of its packaging and it was sealed, so I needed to rip it to open it, and once ripped it's useless so I threw it away."

"But sir, how do you expect us to be able to sell this to another customer without its protective packaging? You wouldn't be happy to buy an item without the packaging would you sir?" he asked.

After five minutes or so we came to a stalemate. He wasn't going to give me a refund, irrespective of the fact that I did in fact want to spend more money on a more expensive item, and I wasn't going to leave the shop without either a full refund or a part-exchange for a better item. Finally he said "Look sir, there is nothing I can do. If I allow this item to be returned to us in this condition I could lose my job as it will have my name on the return; it just cannot go back into stock in that condition, and it's not faulty, so there is nothing I can do!"

What did he say........? It's not faulty, so there's nothing he can do. So that therefore means that if it were faulty, there would be something he could do.

"That's fine", I said, "but the problem is, that it doesn't actually work! I can't make out any picture on the video monitor, so unfortunately I am returning this item as it is faulty."
"Really?" he asked. "But you said you weren't happy with it…"
"That's right," I said, "I'm not happy that it doesn't bloody work!"

Five minutes later, I had my part-exchange and the unnamed shop in question had a "Faulty" item on their hands that wasn't actually faulty, it was just unbelievably crap!

So there we have a lesson in life. Be honest. Be really honest. Failing that, lie.

Wednesday 26th September 2012

Last night it finally happened. We were hoping to hold out until 1st October, but there was no escaping it – the heating had to go on. I dread putting the heating on for the first time. It's the final nail in the coffin for summer, the bills will be rising, and you have to deal with that awful smell when the radiators kick in and burn off all the dust and old spiders that have collected over the summer.

So, depressingly, the heating is on and Christmas is approaching. (Yes I know it's only September, but already there are adverts on the TV and special displays in the shops.) Ladies and Gentlemen, it's time for my annual cut-back.

Every year, around this time, I like to look at what I'm spending and attempt to cut back, in the vain hope that we'll make some savings that we can put towards the winter bills and Christmas, only for me to forget about it a week later and then revive the idea again when the heating gets turned on next year.

I thought I would start as I meant to go on, so first things first, I decided against buying a coffee this morning. I have a long commute and a hot coffee just about gets me through it intact. Ever since I gave up alcohol (I'm sure that will feature in a fun-packed entry in the future) I have become more dependent on another drug – caffeine.

A morning coffee costs me £2.20. Let's work out what that would cost me over the year. I religiously buy a coffee every day. I don't always commute five times a week, however, as I often work from home on Thursdays (and we need to consider the bank holidays.) So lets say, on average, I buy 4.5 coffees a week. I get 28 days holiday, but I only ever take around 20 days a year (sad but true) so let's take 4 weeks off the 52-week year.

So 4.5 x 48 = 216 coffees. That's a lot of coffee. Next we need to find out the annual cost of that coffee. 216 x £2.20 = £475.20. So, if I cut out the coffee, I can save just under £500 a year. That's amazing. Well actually, I need to get real here. £475.20 is actually a good price to pay for the enjoyment I get out of it. I need to consider that without the morning warmth and buzz that I get from my coffee, I would be miserable. I would inevitably turn up to work in a mood, have an argument with my boss and lose my job. Drastic, yes, but entirely possible. That is why this morning I searched the kitchen cupboards for an unused present from 2008. My trusty travel mug!

This morning I made a coffee at home and brought it with me, and it's actually not too bad. Ok, it's not anywhere near as good, it's not as hot, I have to carry it with me everywhere and I have to wash it up every day, but it doesn't cost me £2.20. Although, in order to work out the true savings I would make in a year, I need to work out the cost of the home-made coffee and deduct that from the £475.20.

When drinking the instant variety, I drink Kenco Rich Roast. (Don't judge me, people.) It costs £4.68 for 150 grams. Thanks to some quick research on the internet, and some people that are even sadder than me, I have found out that I can get 74 teaspoons out of 150 grams of coffee. I like my coffee strong, so I use one and a half teaspoons per cup, which totals 49.3, but for the purposes of this, let's call it 50. So a £4.68 jar will buy me 50 coffees. That's not bad. That's amazing actually – it works out at just 9.3p per cup. Except it doesn't. While I've never bothered with sugar, I do like milk, and a very quick calculation gets me to 3p per cup.

So, 216 coffees x 12.3p = £26.56. I then deduct £26.56 from £475.20 to get my total net saving of £448.64.

Ok, that's a lot of work to come up with a figure, and £475 would have done as a rough estimate, but it is nice to know exactly what you could save by just making a small tweak to your daily routine. That £448.64 would probably pay my gas bill over the winter. It's certainly food for thought, and talking about food, that was my next natural step.

I aim to take in some lunch from home every day, but it doesn't quite work out like that and I probably buy lunch at least three times a week. Lunch these days in London costs around £5. For me it consists of a sandwich, wrap or salad, a drink and an accompaniment, whether that be crisps, a granola bar or a piece of fruit. Depending on where I go it could be more or it could be less, but let's say it averages out at £5. So £5 x 3 days x 48 weeks = £720 a year. Without going into the same detail as above, I could make my own lunch each day and it would cost around £1 per day. So £1 x 3 days x 48 weeks = £144. The net saving would be £576.

So in total, this year, I could make two very simple changes to my daily routine and I could save over a thousand pounds per year. That would pay for my winter bills and a good chunk of Christmas. So why am I not that excited about this revelation? Because you know as well as me that this time tomorrow I will be sipping on a shop-bought latte debating whether to buy lunch from M&S or Pret.

Friday 28th September 2012

We have a coffee morning at work this morning. I've been guilty in the past of sniggering at those who partake. I've always assumed it's something that the Women's Institute or the local bowls club get up to. I've always been polite enough to buy a piece of cake and coo and gasp at how light the sponge is or ask just how they got that filling so creamy, because behind all of the pleasantries the main reason for a coffee morning is to raise money, and in most cases, that money goes to charity. Today's coffee morning at work is in aid of the Macmillan nurses, an organisation that really earns its crust.

Put simply, without this organisation hundreds of thousands of people would suffer an extremely painful and lonely death from cancer. Macmillan nurses are there to give cancer patients the home care that they need while suffering their awful illness. I know because right now a family member has terminal cancer and is in their care.

So today, not only have I brought my spare change, I've brought a cake. Yes, brought, not bought! A cake! An actual cake! A cake that I made!

I'm sorry that that last paragraph featured so many short sentences and exclamation marks, but I don't know how else to make clear how remarkable it is that I made a cake! Whilst I enjoy cooking and all of the pleasure that cooking and eating brings, I despise baking. It's all so precise. 150 grams of this, 225 grams of that and if you're one gram out, or if you don't mix the ingredients until both of your arms fall off, you end up with a pancake. (Ironically, one of the few sweet things I actually can make.) This time, however, the problem is not the cake itself – it's how to get it to the office. It's a delicate item – you can't just wrap it up in tin foil and chuck it in a carrier bag. Actually, it turns out you can, as that is exactly what I resorted to after trying and failing to find a container that would fit.

So today I have a bag with me, a carrier bag. I hate having bags. Normally I take four items with me each day. Train pass, wallet, keys and phone. Four items, four pockets, zero bags. The reason I don't like bags is not down to the bag itself, it's down to my own lack of confidence. I don't trust myself to remember that I have it with me and spend the whole journey paranoid that I'll forget it. I joined a gym a few years back and I spent more money replacing my gym kit than I did on the membership itself. What I could never work out was how my property never actually found its way to lost property. Who are the people keeping hold of sweaty and smelly gym clothes? Who thinks to himself "Ok, it's minging now, but I reckon, after a wash, that will go lovely with my black cords."

So right now I am panicking. Partly about the cake, and whether it meets my high standards, but mainly about the bag and the possibility that I might leave it on the train.

I'm not exactly sure how women cope in this situation. They have lots of bags. Lots and lots of bags. I remember when women just had one bag. The rule seemed to be one bag, but no limit on size. The bags got bigger and bigger until one day, I started to see other bags creeping in. Suddenly, there wasn't just a handbag – there was a bag for life, a cotton bag, a little brown bag and every so often, when really desperate, a carrier bag. Not content with this, they went further and we now have rucksacks, normally with the name of a gym on the back, and pull-along cases on wheels. I'm certain that a lot of women carry around more stuff on their morning commute than I would on a six-month round-the-world trip.

In their defence, women do get a rough deal. Women's clothes often don't have pockets and if they do, they look unflattering when filled. Women often wear shoes that are incredibly uncomfortable to walk long distances in, so it is sensible to bring an extra pair, sometimes two, if a gym visit is required. Long hair can be a pain, so there are brushes, lotions, bobbles, bands and hair-ties that need to be considered. Then there's make up – it's not just a case of a bit of powder and mascara, its far more complicated than that – there are toners and moisturisers and bronzers, as well as cotton wool and wipes to consider. I'm a new age man – I understand all of the things a woman needs to consider when coming to work. The thing is, I've also seen a woman's desk and I know that scattered across that desk you will see all of the above. Check under the desk and you will see at least two pairs of shoes. Check the cloakroom or the clothes rack and you will see spare coats, cardigans, dresses and umbrellas.

So I've got an idea. All of those women and, come to think of it, men who come to work like Baa Baa Black sheep (three bags full) should today clear their desks of all of their old junk. Chuck it away. Put all of the stuff you do carry around with you on, in and under your desk. You are now free of your bags. The trains will be able to take more passengers and suddenly we have solved the problem of lost property.

Speaking of which, if anyone did find a Reebok rucksack containing a sweaty t-shirt and shorts on the 18:12 from Euston in the spring of 2007, it was mine; contact details are at the back of the book.

Monday 1st October 2012

My daughter is now of the age where she can make decisions. They are not always sensible, in fact sometimes they don't make any sense, but she now has the requisite brainpower to think and, consequently, decide. Most weekends, we ask her what she wants to do and she thinks for a moment and then says something like "I'd like to go to the baker's", or "I'd like to wash the car". While practical and, particularly in the case of the latter, necessary, they don't exactly make for a fun-filled afternoon out.

What usually happens in this situation is that we say, "Shall we go to the farm instead?" or "Would you prefer to go to the park?" and she jumps about, gets excited, we get our things and off to the farm or park we go. Not this weekend. This weekend we asked our daughter what she would like to do and she said five words which, even now, send shivers down my spine.

"I'd like to go swimming", she said.
"Shall we go to the farm instead?" I asked.
"No, swimming", she said.
"Would you prefer to go to the park?" I asked.

"No, I'd like to go swimming, Daddy."

This was the first time she had ever come up with a sensible suggestion, and certainly the first time she had decided she wanted to go swimming. For the first 18 months of her life my wife took her to swimming lessons where she spent the whole 30 minutes either crying, pooing or sleeping and amazingly, every so often, a combination of all three. While I wanted my daughter to be able to swim and at the very least be confident in the water, I couldn't help but feel slightly pleased that I wouldn't ever have to take her swimming.

You might think I'm being a misery, but I hate going swimming. Before we start, I'd best clarify what I mean by 'going swimming'.

Actual swimming, I love. I enjoy the feeling of the water trickling through my fingers as I glide along. I love the feeling of weightlessness. I love the fact that when you go underwater, the world stops for a moment, your vision is blurred and your hearing is reduced to muffled noises; it's just so quiet and peaceful. Swimming on holiday is fantastic – it's generally done in the open air, you have the sun on your back and there's an endless supply of ice cream nearby – what's not to love about swimming?

'Going swimming' is very different. On holiday you tend to do other things, and the swimming happens naturally in between all of the other stuff. It's the filler. It's the staple. To use an analogy, if you were looking at a plate of food, swimming on holiday would be the humble potato. It's readily available, not wildly exciting, but you'd miss it if you didn't have it.

So 'going swimming' for me while not on holiday is like being force-fed a huge plate of potato, but as if that's not enough, I have to eat it in front of strangers, while sitting in my underpants.

I woke up on Saturday morning with visions of fluffy bunny rabbits, cute sheep and a dog called Barney. That to me is fun. Throwing on an old jumper and going down to the farm to feed the animals. Watching the children's faces as they stroke the animals. As soon as it starts to rain, off to the shop for coffee and cake. But not this time. Instead I get to see people called Dawn and Tony, 90% naked, shouting and smacking their offspring. I get to watch a dysfunctional family play out their sorry lives in front of me, like a very wet episode of Jeremy Kyle. I'd like to say that it's all worth it, that seeing the smile on my wonderful daughter's face makes everything ok, but it doesn't, because her smile is hidden by the snot that is streaming from her nose.

To make matters worse, we went to a 'splash pool'. Essentially, what this means is you can do everything, except swim. There are floats, flumes, slides, whirlpools and rapids. Every twenty minutes an alarm goes off, which when I was a child meant that Smelly Simon had just proved once again how he got his nickname, but apparently nowadays it signals the start of a tsunami. Wave after wave comes tumbling towards the shallow end, knocking over every toddler and pregnant lady that stands in its path. Unfortunately my final destination is near and so I haven't got time to share with you the baffling parking system, the awful changing-room experience, the pre-pubescent lifeguards or the science experiment that they call food.

I'm glad my daughter had fun on Saturday and I'm truly glad that she got to choose what she wanted to do. Next week, she will be choosing again. She will be choosing between the farm and the park.

Tuesday 2nd October 2012

As a commuter, I have my routines. All commuters have their routines. They generally take the same route to the station, at the same time, buy the same coffee, get the same paper, stand in the same place and sit in the same seat.

I'm lucky enough to get a seat every time on the morning leg of my commute, no doubt to the frustration of other commuters. What they have to remember, however, is that my commute is longer than theirs and therefore far more expensive. I would actually far rather stand all the way for a journey half as long and a ticket that costs half as much. That said, I chose to live as far out as I do and so can't really complain.

When I started writing this book, however, I found that I had to change one of my own routines. I had to change where I sat. Choosing your seat on a train is a delicate operation and there are many things that need to be factored in to the decision. You have to weigh up the fact that the front of the train will be busier, but you'll be first off the train and therefore first out of the station. The back of the train will be quieter, but on a 12-car train, it's a hell of a walk at the other end. I therefore decided on the middle of the train as it is moderately busy and has a moderate walk at the destination point; the only real downside was the fact that the toilets were so close. You might think that being near toilets is a good thing, but being within 200 metres of train toilets is not a good thing, it's a danger to your health.

My usual seat of choice was a table seat, by the window in the middle of the train. The table offers a flat surface on which to read a paper or use the iPad. When I started to write this book I noticed I had a problem, as people were reading what I was writing. You might think "What's the big deal?" but it is incredibly off-putting. Can you imagine trying to write a dissertation with a total stranger reading every word over your shoulder? I also had the problem that my 'dissertation' could well feature said stranger, and if that were the case, it wouldn't be congratulating them on their good hygiene or their exemplary manners. So essentially, I had to move. It was a difficult thing to do and an even more difficult choice to make. I needed a seat that meant I wasn't overlooked, but also meant it wasn't too busy or too far to walk. I eventually found the perfect seat. Well, almost perfect.

There is a seat in most trains that sits alone. It has plenty of leg-room, a giant window and zero chance of anyone looking over your shoulder. The seat I am sitting on right now is effectively in a corridor where people can secure their bikes. No major problem there you might think, but it is also right next to the toilet. Now I'm not wishing to be dramatic here, but I need to explain exactly how close to the toilet I am. I am close enough that I can open the door without getting up. People often assume I am the toilet attendant. People come out of the toilet and the slightest bump or jolt sends them sprawling across my lap. I am so close that I can't just smell the fumes, I can taste them.

Strangely though, I love my new seat. I love watching people's toilet habits and find them fascinating. I've become something of a toilet expert. "You need to press the yellow one that's flashing to open the doors, you then need to press the green one inside to close the door, and don't forget to press the red one to lock it." When there's a queue, I seem to have become the conductor, explaining to people approximately how long the wait is and giving them insights into the noises that are coming from inside. "That's the flush just gone there, and that's the sound of the hand dryer; shouldn't be long now." Every so often, when the toilets are out of order, I get abuse too. Not directly, but when I politely explain that there is no point in waiting because the toilet isn't working, I often get a barrage of swear-words thrown in my direction.

One thing I have noticed and had never realised is that people actually do poo on trains. Now I know I mentioned about the smell earlier, but I had always assumed the smell was down to the fact that these trains run late into the night and often have to cope with inebriated travellers and perhaps are just poorly maintained, but no, some commuters actually use train toilets to have their morning poo. I haven't managed to find anyone that's established this as part of their morning routine, but it seems there are plenty who have absolutely no qualms with taking in the morning paper and doing their business.

I have always had a fear of using public toilets and to this day, I'm still not able to do 'number twos' in a public loo. On the rare occasion that I have had no choice, I am ashamed to say I have had to use the disabled toilet. I need to be locked away in my own room. I'm sorry to be blunt here, but I cannot stand the sound, let alone the smell, of other people shitting and I would hate other people to be subjected to my business too.

To me, it's a very personal thing – it is certainly not a public outing. Public cubicles in my mind should all have a sign reading "Absolute Emergency Only". They should have a spring loaded door, so that they only open if people are charging through them at more than 30 mph. Routine pooers should be banned. Those that look at their watch and think "Oh, it's 11 o'clock – I'd best empty my bowels." No sir, wait until you get home and do it in private, I want neither to hear it nor smell it.

I know that a lot of people must feel the same as me because at work, there are the people that I've nicknamed 'the cats'. These are people who come down from other floors to crap in our toilets. They are clearly embarrassed and don't want to be recognised. It is often said that cats don't crap on their own doorstep, often preferring to poo in other people's gardens. Generally, it is accepted that this is because they are clean animals and they don't want to live in their own mess. I think it's because, like me, they are disgusted and embarrassed by the whole thing and they just want a bit of bloody privacy.

Wednesday 3rd October 2012

This morning I woke up late. I'm not exactly sure how I managed it, considering the alarm was set for the same time as every other day this year, and of course the time on the clock itself is set 20 minutes fast in the vain hope that it will trick me into thinking it's later than it actually is. Why do I still persevere with that ridiculous tactic? All it does is cause more confusion than is necessary at that time in the morning. This morning I woke up late because of a condition that I have. I suffer from sleep snoozing. Somehow, in my sleep, I manage to hit that big black button on the top of the alarm clock, without any knowledge of doing it. Those that suffer from sleep walking have my sympathy, but spare a thought for those, like me, that sleep snooze. Those that sleep walk may suffer once every few weeks. I suffer eight or nine times a day and there are only nine minutes or so between each of my episodes. Who on earth came up with the nine minute snooze setting? Which boffin was scratching his head one day thinking, "Eight minutes, that's barely a nap. Ten minutes, no, that's a full-on sleep. Nine minutes, now that's a snooze!"?

I hate being late. I'm one of these people who aren't late, ever. Even, like today, when I get up late, I'm able to make up the time and get to my destination on time. The only time I am ever late is when the situation is completely out of my control, and that is usually down to someone jumping under the train I'm on, or 100,000 other people being on the same road as me. Not content with just not being late, I have to be early. I'm always early. Even my bloody hair has fallen out early.

When travelling, the trickier the journey, the earlier I tend to leave. I've adopted a strange rule that seems to be to leave 15 minutes earlier for every stage of the journey. If going by car, every motorway will have 15 minutes added for traffic. If travelling by train, 15 minutes added for each change. I went up to Inverness last year which involved getting six different trains. I ended up getting to Inverness before the train did.

Being early can have its advantages. If you turn up early to a gig, you can generally stand nearer the front. Turn up early to a food buffet and you are guaranteed the freshly cooked stuff. There are other situations where being early completely sucks though. Turn up early for an appointment and you have a hell of a wait. An early death can have obvious disadvantages. Book your holiday early and you'll spend most of it on the verge of suicide as every other holidaymaker tells you just how cheap their holiday was because of how late they booked it. Turning up early to a pub is an extremely unpleasant experience. There is nothing that shouts "Loser" more than rocking up on your own, ordering your sad little drink and getting on with the crossword.

So it's an awful shame that I have spent the last fifteen years turning up early to pubs. All of my friends, every single one of them, have spent fifteen years turning up late. When you turn up early and the people you are meeting turn up late, a potential twenty minute wait turns into forty. A long time to wait in most environments, even longer in a pub, but longer still in a pub when England are playing and you are trying to hold eight front-row seats. There is only so long that one person can hold onto eight seats in a busy pub, but when you combine that with England and a World Cup, that time diminishes rapidly. When the football isn't on, I would say it's around thirty minutes. When the football is on, it could be as little as ten.

Firstly, a group of people will enquire as to whether the seats are free; I will state that my friends will be along in a minute, knowing full well it will be at least forty. I then spend five minutes spreading all of my possessions around the table. Nothing is wasted. The Evening Standard gets spread out across the table and if I'm lucky, I might have a supplement too. I'll then hang my coat on the chair next to me; my jumper on the one opposite and even my pen will be tactically placed.

What happens next is like a scene from a wildlife documentary, where the cackle of hyenas team up to prize away the lions' latest kill. The only thing worse than having to watch the game from the car park is having to keep bumping into the bullies every time I go to the bar or the toilet. Even the poor old lion doesn't have to put up with the indignity of facing the hyenas every time they go for a piss.

It's often said that it's better to be late in this world than early in the next, and while I agree with the sentiment, I won't be changing my habits. Being early has its down-sides while booking holidays or attending appointments, but being early can also be absolutely bloody spectacular. I urge you, some day soon, to set the alarm, get down to the coast, or failing that somewhere high up, and watch the beauty of the sunrise. It's something that those who are late will always be missing out on.

Friday 5th October 2012

While it's true that I don't believe in superstitions, I do try wherever possible to avoid walking under ladders. But this is on the grounds of safety, rather than any possible bad luck. However, since becoming a father, I suppose I have become a little more superstitious. There are times when our little girl is sleeping well and I will attempt to mention it to my wife and she will say "Ssshhhh, don't say it!" The belief is that if you mention it, you will 'jinx' it and suddenly, without warning the thing you want to happen, suddenly won't, or the thing you don't want to happen, suddenly will, or in this case, the thing that actually is happening, suddenly won't be. It's amazing really just how sophisticated this superstition is.

Thanks largely to my wife I now employ this utterly ridiculous tactic in almost every aspect of my life. When on the motorway, I sometimes start to think how wonderfully traffic free the road is, but then I hear my wife's words in my head – "Ssshhhh, you'll jinx it!" When my football team of choice are winning, I start to think how great the three points will be and exactly where that might put us in the table, when suddenly I hear my wife's words once again, loud and clear.

The problem with this ridiculous superstition is that by not saying it, you actually make things worse for yourself because instead of saying it and moving on, you are left with this thought that is bouncing around in your head, desperate to get out. Thoughts have a natural outlet – it's called speech. Things come into being in your brain and they go out via the mouth, normally through an 'embarrassment filter' – a filter that can process the thought and work out whether it should be shared in the current company. This filter is quite sensitive, however, and is often impaired by alcohol, stupidity or both.

On Wednesday it's fair to say that I 'jinxed' myself. I made the bold statement that I am never late.

Today, I am late.

It was, however, completely out of my control. On Fridays my mother-in-law looks after our daughter, and every Friday she drives at 83mph down winding country lanes in order to arrive on our driveway approximately three to four minutes late. It's normally nothing a little jog to the station can't fix.

Today however she was fifteen minutes late and it wasn't down to the traffic or the car; it was down to the weather. The relentless wind and rain through the night had managed to uproot a tree and deposit it across the main road that links her house to ours.

I couldn't work out what was more annoying, as I lightly jogged down the road to the station. Was it the litres of water that were being splashed up my leg every time so much as a milk float passed me by, or was it the conkers that were flying towards me at both head and groin height? My decision was made easy in the end, as I crossed the road and a bus roared passed to ensure I was soaked evenly on both sides. As a pedestrian, I think October has got to be one of the most dangerous months. Sure January and February can get slippery, but in October we have to deal with flying conkers, crazy umbrella owners and the tricky job of walking on slippery leaves and spent conker shells. This morning I feel like those two burglars in Home Alone.

Eventually I got to the station, bought a coffee and stood at my normal place on the platform. I hadn't realised that as I was on a later train and there are fewer people to accommodate, the train has fewer carriages. (The train people like to dress it up and say the train is a 'shorter formation'.) The end of the train was now thirty metres to my left and I had to run to make sure that I got on. Running for me is never going to come naturally, but running with a coffee in one hand and an inside-out umbrella in the other is a skill that even the greatest monks have yet to master.

So now, finally, I'm on a train and I'm dry. I just hope we don't get delayed!

Bugger, I think I've just 'jinxed' it…

Monday 8th October 2012

This weekend I decided to make a complaint.

This may sound innocuous to you, run-of-the-mill even, but for me this is genuine progress. I have ambled through the last 33 years on this planet, totally unable to complain. No matter what a shoddy experience I might have, or what terrible service I might receive, I'll smile politely, keep quiet and pay the bill. As soon as I'm in the car, my wife, family or friends will then get a full run-down of exactly what was wrong and exactly how they should improve.

I am a closet complainant, happy to moan, but doing so behind closed doors and out of earshot. Cold food? Sloppy service? Rude staff? Boy, are they going to get it in the car on the way home. I'm not sure why I'm like this. I'm quite confident in normal every day life. Sometimes too confident for my own good. A celebrity only needs to be within five square miles and I'll be able to seek them out for a little chat about what they're up to and what they have in the pipeline.

You sometimes hear celebrities say things like "Oh no, people are very respectful, I rarely get people just walking up to me in the street." Maybe I didn't get the memo. I can count at least ten times in the past where I have just introduced myself, said I was a fan of their work and then gone on to have a lovely chat. I have a rule of not disturbing them if they are chatting with others, or if they are eating, but if they are just sitting there or standing there, then that's fair game. My most recent chat was with Dame Kelly Holmes on this very train. She sat down opposite me and we got off the train together, so I wasn't going to turn down that opportunity. We actually had some common ground too, in the very broadest sense. It was leading up to the 2012 Olympics and she was obviously heavily involved and so was I. Well, sort of. I was a 'Gamesmaker' for the Olympics and during our chat she seemed genuinely excited and proud of the volunteers and she wished me luck for the games. If I'm honest, it seemed a bit surreal that a Dame and double gold-medallist was wishing me good luck for the upcoming Olympic Games.

There was another time that I approached a couple of celebrities and I realise now, looking back, that the celebrities in question must have been terrified. Firstly, I was under the influence of alcohol. I wasn't drunk; I was just very well lubricated. Secondly, it was dark. Thirdly, they were in a blacked-out Range Rover. (Thinking back, I've no idea how I spotted them given those three factors.) And lastly, because I wasn't 100% sure it was them, I circled the car four times.

So, picture the scene. It's a dark, cold, winter's night. Two celebrities are parked up at the side of the road in a blacked-out vehicle and a scruffy drunk is circling the car. (It was also a Friday and dress-down day involved me not only relaxing my dress code, but my facial hair too.)

Suddenly, the scruffy drunk approaches the car and knocks on the passenger-side window. After a lengthy discussion between the two and a second knock from the scruffy drunk, the electric motor kicks in and the window is slowly lowered and in a broad Geordie accent, Dec from Ant and Dec asks if he can help me, with Ant from Ant and Dec looking on.

I had spent so long trying to figure out if it was them and building up the courage to speak to them that when it came to actually saying something, I had completely dried up. After what seemed like ten minutes I finally managed to say something, and to this day I still go bright red at the thought of it. "So you really are friends outside of work then."

That was it!

I had knocked on the window of a blacked-out car and disturbed two celebrities, (who were both chatting and eating, thus breaking both of my own silly rules,) in order to state that these two very nice gentlemen are indeed friends. Thinking back now, I'm annoyed I didn't make reference to the fact that, even in a car, Ant was on the left and Dec was on the right!

Annoyingly, my encounter with the pint-sized Geordie duo wasn't my most embarrassing celebrity moment. A year or two later I was walking hand-in-hand with my wife through Camden when I spotted TV's Stephen Mangan, and proceeded to confidently smile, wave and say hello. Well, that's how it now goes in my head as I try desperately to erase the memory of pointing at him and saying "Look, it's him, off of........" as he politely smiled and waved and said "Yes, it's me, off of ......" and continued walking. He knew that I couldn't think where I knew him from, but he just rolled with it. He wasn't embarrassed at all.

Stephen Mangan is in that awkward category where he is famous, but not really famous. I imagine people point or stare, trying to work out where they know him from. Is he famous? Did I work with him once? Is he a friend of Stan's? For those of you that have now Googled Stephen Mangan, yes, he is that bloke that was in Green Wing, Alan Partridge and Episodes. And yes, he is a bit strange looking.

So, we've established I'm confident and stupid in equal measure, but still unable to complain, until this weekend that is. We visited some friends of ours and went to a beautiful park. The park has gardens, a museum and a lovely restaurant. After spending a good while in the children's play-park, watching our children swing, slide and climb their way to exhaustion, we retired to the restaurant for some much-needed refreshment.

It was rustic, home-cooked food and the hand-made burger and chunky chips fitted the bill perfectly. Mine was fantastic. It was hot, tasty and completely devoid of sharp plastic objects. My wife's burger on the other hand managed the first two, but failed on the last. The object in question was extremely hard and sharp. It was by pure luck that my wife managed to pluck it from her mouth before it did any real damage. Who knows what it was or how it got in there, but it was certainly time for me to man up in front of my friends. I told them that it wasn't right and we should complain. They agreed. We should speak to either the manager or the chef. They agreed.

To my surprise one of our friends Nic, took the initiative and asked the waitress if the chef could please come out to speak to us. That's fine, I thought. She's taken care of the admin; it's time for me to take care of the business. Ten minutes later there was no chef and no manager. I now had an issue. I was already highly stressed about having to complain, but now, there is a second complaint that needs discussing. I've now got to complain about the wait to speak to the manager as well as the original complaint. This is like asking someone who is afraid of flying to board a plane and then, halfway through, telling them that it's their turn to fly it.

Ten minutes later and we still had not been visited by either the chef or the manager. It is at this point that my daughter asked to go to the toilet and as she is only two and a half, she needed some assistance. I am ashamed to admit that I took the bait. I've never been so happy to accompany my daughter to the loo.

"I'll go!" I shouted, as I grabbed her hand and skipped off to the toilet. Needless to say, by the time I got back, the situation had been resolved. Our good friend Jay managed to explain, very articulately, I'm told, exactly what they needed to do in terms of improving their customer care. The sharp, plastic item was presented to the manager and he apologised accordingly. We later received free coffee and cake by way of apology and everyone seemed to be happy. Everyone except me. My coffee was cold and my cake was stale.

Boy, did they hear about that in the car on the way home!

Tuesday 9th October 2012

Since I started this book I have had to get used to establishing a new routine. I am someone who generally welcomes change with open arms. I think my attitude towards change is down to my school days, where I constantly had to deal with it. Firstly, while at school you have to deal with your body going through changes. I had to deal with my voice getting lower, my face getting spottier, my legs getting longer and my body getting hairier.

Changing teachers meant that I had to get used to a new set of rules, new guidelines and boundaries. The things that made you good or bad in one teacher's eyes were not the same for another. I was a well-behaved child at school, but never a top achiever. I was always in the top set, but I generally achieved average results. I never misbehaved, but I often got bored, so my time in the classroom was often spent trying to make other people laugh, with varying degrees of success. Often, in order to split up a group of chatty children, the teacher would move you around and sit you next to other people. This didn't really work in my case, as it just gave me a new audience to try my material out on.

School days provided an endless stream of change; every other day you would change best friends, every few weeks you would change your underwear, every few months you would change hairstyle and every few years you would have to up sticks and change schools.

And then in order to write this book I had to make a change. Instead of reading the paper or listening to a podcast, I started to write. It's extremely enjoyable and I'm annoyed that I didn't do it sooner. I find that I am more creative and ideas are far more free-flowing in the morning, so my routine tends to be to write on the morning commute and then, after a long day's work, I spend the evening commute going over what I have written and editing it where necessary. I have found that the nine-hour gap in between writing and re-reading gives me sufficient time to make judgements on whether something is unnecessary, boring or simply doesn't work.

The one problem with this new routine is that it means I can no longer catch up with the news. No more morning paper, no more Evening Standard on the way home, and no more podcasts. A few years ago I couldn't get enough news, but now, with a young daughter, news is harder to come by as time is very precious. I tend to spend my daughter's waking hours keeping her happy. That will generally involve going to the park, playing with wooden kitchen items or watching Peppa Pig. No chance of catching up with the news there. I then spend her sleeping hours doing mundane things like cooking, eating and tidying up after her. In terms of this book, having a lack of knowledge of the news is actually quite good. It would be far too easy to comment on the news each day, but I have two main reasons for not doing that.

Firstly, that's what journalists are there for, and even if I did try to put a comical slant on it, that space is currently filled by comedians and I am neither a journalist nor a comedian, (as I'm sure you'll agree).

Secondly, by commenting on the news, I will be dating this book. Who wants to read this book in ten years' time and read about some boring politician who was having an affair with his wife's sister's yoga instructor?

This morning, however, I did manage to catch five minutes of news. On a Monday and

Tuesday, it's my job to get our daughter ready and take her to the child-minder. Most mornings, while eating breakfast, and in an attempt to keep her still while trying to put her shoes on with one hand and brush her hair with the other, we watch some child-friendly telly. This morning, my daughter spotted my iPad. Now, sorry to dispel the magic, people, I don't use a fancy laptop or Mac and I don't use any fancy word processing software, I simply use my iPad and the application called Notes. (For those of you reading this in the year 2020, an iPad was a small touch-screen device. Yes, we had to touch the screen with our fingers! How terribly old-fashioned!)

After spotting the iPad my daughter insisted that she wanted to play with it. A few days earlier, in an effort to keep her happy while eating out with friends, I had downloaded a game called Peppa Pig's Party Time. Initially, I was unwilling, due to the proximity of the milk, but I soon realised that if she were playing the game, then the telly would be free for me to take in some much-needed news.

After just two minutes I wished I hadn't. What I didn't realise is that the last few weeks haven't just been news-free for me, they have been bad news free, and that is a good thing. The last few weeks have proved once and for all that no news is definitely good news! How often have we turned on the news, only to be subjected to a seemingly endless barrage of depressing stories?

I think they should rename the news and call it 'Bad News'. To counter that, they should also create a totally new programme and call it 'Good News'. They could run one after the other and so the viewer would have the choice of watching just the good news, just the bad news, or both.

Now I know what these pesky broadcasters are like with their viewing figures, so I can't see the 'Bad News' format getting past the executives, but I think it could work. What if the world of news broadcasting finally found its way to the 21st-Century viewer and introduced an interactive element to the start of each broadcast?

Red buttons at the ready, everyone. What would you like first, the good news or the bad?

Wednesday 10th October 2012

This morning I noticed the first hat and the first pair of gloves of this winter. Officially it's still autumn, but this morning it feels incredibly wintry as there's a crisp frost underfoot and plumes of steam escaping from the mouths of all of the commuters.

It marked a special occasion for me, as I have added my first layer since spring. For the last few weeks, everyone else at the station has been wearing a combination of jumpers, jackets, blazers and coats; I have continued to wear nothing but a thin cotton shirt. Ok, it might be polyester, but let's move on. I hate wearing layers and avoid it whenever possible. The problem with wearing layers when you commute is that it's essentially extra baggage that needs carrying around, whether on your back, in your arms or stuffed in your bag. Trains have become relatively advanced in recent years, with the welcome inclusion of air-conditioning for the summer and heating for the winter.

Air-conditioning during the summer is fantastic. You arrive at the train hot and bothered, board the train and within a few minutes you start to cool down, genuinely appreciative of the cooling facilities on offer. The problem with trains in the winter is that there only seem to be two heat settings, and they tend to be 'Off' and 'Surface of the Sun'. Today it's been set to the latter.

As everyone boards the train, hats, gloves, coats, jumpers, blazers and jackets are removed in unison in an attempt to acclimatise to the train's ridiculously high heat setting. There really doesn't seem any point in having heating on trains. People have dressed warmly for the weather and are generally rather snug in their chosen extra layers. Even with no heating at all, the train would be far warmer than the outside temperature due to the body heat of the passengers, and people could just regulate their own temperature by layering and de-layering accordingly.

Banning heating on trains would almost certainly save money on electricity or fuel and I'm certain that lost property would be reduced as people would tend to de-layer less often, therefore keeping their possessions about their person. I'm certain I've made up the word de-layer, but having used it three times in the last three sentences I'm warming to it, (pun definitely not intended,) so it's staying.

As I've said, I'm not a fan of bringing unnecessary items, like warm clothes, to work and I try to travel as light as possible. I'm normally able to go until late October, sometimes early November, without the addition of so much as a jumper. I'm aware of how ridiculous this is and I'm reminded just what a fool I am on those mornings when my skin ends up matching the colour of the sky-blue shirt that I'm wearing.

On mornings when it's extremely cold, I tend to jog in an effort to get to my destination a little quicker and to raise my body temperature just a little. So, with a coffee spilling and splashing about due to a combination of the motion of the jogging and the slipping and sliding on the leaves and conkers under foot, I get to the station both layer-less, (another new layer-based word,) and coffee-less.

October the 10th is extremely early for me to be adding a jumper to my morning commute and I am still likely to use the jogging technique from time to time, until it's time to upgrade to the winter coat. Like a seasoned explorer, I like to use nature as my guide. When the last tree has shed its last leaf, it's time. Even my winter coat is a fairly light affair. It finishes at the waist, has no hood and has relatively little padding. It's effectively a zip-up jumper with pockets.

Having written that last sentence, I'm annoyed to realise that a zip-up jumper with pockets is effectively a fleece, and with two or three fleeces in my possession, I could have been using them all along, thus saving money on the purchase of a coat and the extra few grams of weight on my back.

As I look down the train, I can see passengers starting to stand up and commence the process of layering; we must be close to our destination, and that is my cue to finish today's chapter.

It looks a beautiful morning in London. If only I didn't have my jumper, I'd quite fancy a light morning jog.

Friday 12th October 2012

Today the tables have turned; the roles have been reversed; we have indeed come full circle. Today I am taking my dad to the football. I've been to the football plenty of times *with* my dad, but I've always been of the opinion that he is taking me. Even well into adulthood, and with me able to pay my own way, it was my dad that was taking me to the football, rather than the other way around.

I've always had a close relationship with my dad and as I grew up to love sport and then, later on, alcohol, we grew closer and closer. My mum has always said that while my brother inherited my dad's humour and looks, I inherited his love for sport and his temper. Thanks dad.

My dad spent quite a lot of time trying and failing to convert my brother to sport. My brother was into his music and sport just didn't interest him. When you look back through family albums you invariably get at least one photo in either a school sports kit or some sort of fake football top from the market, but not in my brother's case. It was just an endless succession of jeans and Iron Maiden t-shirts.

The nearest my brother got to school sports was when he had to run for the bus in the morning, and even then the long hair, the ankle-length trench-coat and the smoke-filled lungs managed to slow him down to a light jog.

As soon as I was old enough to make my own decisions, and with the pressure off, I naturally fell into sport. I got into most of the school sports teams, never being the star, but able to hold my own, and I could see that my dad was proud.

One of my happiest childhood memories, which I still play back in my mind now, is when I scored my first goal in front of my dad. I remember it so clearly. We were playing against Francis Coombe, which, in a strange twist is where my dad used to go to school. Francis Coombe were the worst team in the district at the time, closely followed by us, so it was an opportunity to score a rare goal. The team sheet had gone up the day before and my dad had confirmed that he was coming along to watch; I couldn't wait.

Twenty minutes into the game and dad still hadn't arrived; I had already hit the post and I was sure that he had forgotten. Hitting the post was an impressive achievement on our school pitch as they tended to move in the wind and had the diameter of a toothpick.

My stomach was churning and I spent longer looking at the entrance to the school field than I did at the ball. Finally, I saw him coming down the path and, in an amazing piece of timing, he arrived behind the goal at the same time that I got put through, one-on-one with the keeper. My legs were like jelly, I had no idea what to do, so I just smashed it. The keeper went down early and the ball rifled into the middle of the goal. My dad isn't one for emotions, but the nod and the thumbs-up told me that he was proud. A very happy memory for me.

When playing football for your school team, there is a certain pressure to support a good football team. When I was at school, Manchester United were just becoming popular again due to them winning the league for the first time in twenty-six years, and Liverpool had a rich history, so most kids went for one or the other. I however, was happy to be a Watford fan. To me, it was an easy choice to make. I lived in Watford, my dad supported Watford, so a Watford fan I became. The advantage of supporting a local team is that you can actually go and watch them play; the disadvantages are the food-poisoning and pneumonia. I remember coming in on Monday mornings and telling and my friends about the games. I loved seeing the envy on their faces. Of course, being kids, they didn't say, "Wow, it sounds great, nice one!", they simply said "Watford are shit, you gaylord."

So today, my dad and I are going to the football, but this time not to see Watford, to see England. I received an email a few weeks ago, inviting me to buy tickets for the price of £20.12. A strange price you might think, but as I had been involved as a volunteer at the recent Olympics, the email explained that "As a show of our appreciation, we would like to offer you tickets at this special price." I took them up on the offer and, having read Wednesday's Evening Standard, so did 7,999 others. The Standard wrote "The London 2012 Olympic 'Games Makers' have again been offered tickets at the promotional price of £20.12, with 8,000 volunteers taking up the offer."

The story also confirmed that tonight's game is a sell-out, which is impressive considering the opposition is San Marino, one of the lowest-ranked teams in the world. To be fair San Marino has a population of just over 30,000. That's the same population as Hitchin, a small town in Hertfordshire. Hardly fair is it – England versus Hitchin?

I'm really looking forward to tonight – a game of football, a catch-up with dad, a bout of food-poisoning and a touch of pneumonia. Perfect. Just like the good old days, with the welcome exclusion of people claiming that England are shit and that I am a gaylord.

Monday 15th October 2012

I managed to travel on the train this weekend without writing a chapter of this book. I was unsure as to whether I should, as my promise was to write something on every train journey, but as this journey was for pleasure and not business, and I promised to write on my commute, I decided that it didn't qualify.

Instead I bought a paper. It's the first time in a month that I've been able to enjoy a morning paper. After about thirty minutes, I came to the conclusion that I wasn't missing much as, once again, story after story seemed to concentrate on murders, abductions and general political incompetence. The only really interesting thing in the paper was the write-up about England and how they had performed against San Marino and that was the one thing I didn't need updating on as I was there to witness it.

I really do think that with the technology available to us nowadays, they should stop printing papers. It's old-fashioned, it's bad for the environment, and on the tube it's downright annoying.

I personally think papers should only exist in the virtual world and be solely downloadable on the various handheld phones and tablets that are available. The name would have to change as you couldn't call them papers anymore; they would probably have to be called 'Downloads' or 'News Updates'. I admit that there are a few things we would need to iron out as not everyone has the ability to access these digital downloads, but I think that gives us an opportunity to kill two birds with one stone.

Every time I see a politician on the telly, they go on about two things: the current financial crisis and the environment. By banning papers we could help both. Banning papers would reduce both emissions from the production and the landfill from the waste. We could also help ease the financial crisis, as it would mean everyone without a suitable device would be tempted to buy one, thus boosting the economy. It's a win-win. The only true losers are the cute fluffy rabbits, who will no longer have anything to line their hutches.

Obviously these digital downloads already exist, but the quality is varied and the fact that only a certain percentage of people use them means that they are not the top priority for the news corporations. Banning papers would ensure that all of the money and effort went into producing the best possible content.

I also think that it should be possible to do a 'pick and mix' and effectively create your own news. The problem with a paper is that many pages go unread, as they try to target everyone with one paper. Is a sixteen year-old student going to be interested in the same things as a sixty year-old accountant? Ok, maybe if that student is studying accountancy, but you understand the point I'm trying to make. By doing a 'pick and mix' you can choose the news that interests you. So I, for instance, wouldn't have to read the stories about fashion or music. Never again would I be told what is 'On Point', and never again would I utter the words "What's the point?"

Newspapers often do giveaways such as CDs, and even this could be carried over to the digital version. Once you have bought the digital download, you could qualify to download the latest single from Plan C, Nemo or Kanye East. Never again, when selling a car, would you have to clear the glove-box of cardboard sleeves with titles like 'Lazy Sunday' or 'The ultimate chill-out'.

The paper I read this weekend had a giveaway, one that I actually may use. Jamie Oliver is releasing a new book and there were two recipe cards enclosed. Last Christmas I received Jamie's latest cookery book and I was genuinely impressed with it. I used it quite a few times and still do now, in fact the only thing that is wrong with it is the title. It's called 'Jamie's 30 Minute Meals', whereas in fact it should be titled 'Jamie's 50 Minute Meals', or more accurately, 'Jamie's Meals in Just Under an Hour'. There are some excellent recipes that are simple and tasty, but you not only have to factor in the extra time it takes to cook, you always have to make an extra trip to the shops in order to find those essential puy lentils or mung beans.

So, Christmas is on its way and Jamie has a new book out and who can blame him, the boy's got to eat. It's called 'Jamie's 15 Minute Meals', or as I've decided to call it, 'Jamie's Meals in about Half an Hour, but You Have to Factor in the Extra Time to Get to the Shops and Back, so Let's Call it an Hour'.

Not as snappy, but far more accurate.

Tuesday 16th October 2012

Last night I happened to catch an advert for the latest iPhone and it annoyed me. In case you are unfamiliar with the iPhone adverts, they essentially walk you through a few features, or sometimes they show you what can be done when you download certain apps. Want to tumble-dry your washing while riding a bike? There's an app for that..... That kind of thing.

Yesterday's advert centred on the headphones and it went something like this: "Everyone's ears are different, none of them are round, why would anyone possibly think of manufacturing round earphones? Look at ours – aren't they great? They're ear-shaped."

A brilliant idea. Ear-shaped earphones. Well done, Apple. The thing is, before they came up with the ear-shaped earphone, they were selling their products complete with the terribly old-fashioned round earphones. So effectively their new marketing campaign is saying: "I know we were lazy before, pedalling our product with inferior spherical accessories, but look, we've finally bothered to look at the issue and we think we've sorted it out."

Strange, isn't it, that they are quite happy to create a marketing campaign that effectively points out that they got it wrong before? You only have to look at how washing powders have evolved over the last ten years to see this in action. It used to be quite simple – you made your choice based on price, and every product simply claimed to be able to wash your clothes better than the others.

Nowadays, every few months, a different brand comes up with a different claim. Firstly there was the temperature debate. "Washing at fifty degrees? Our product works at forty!" Then the following week another company would say: "Forty? No no no, with ours you can wash at thirty." At this rate it won't be long before our washing machines resemble Slush Puppy dispensers.

It's not just temperature – it's the endless claims they make with strange-sounding phrases such as 'actilift', 'anti-bobble' and 'colour care'. If they thought they could get away with it, I'm sure they would happily sneak on preposterous claims such as 'with cancer-curing properties' or 'complete with anti-ageing effect'.

With food, you often see the words 'New and Improved' quoted either on the advert or by the person voicing the advert. I am certain that in 99% of the cases, nothing is new and nothing has been improved, it's just exactly the same as before. All that has happened is they have managed to save up enough money to create another ad campaign, to make yet another failed bid to gain that tiny extra little bit of market-share, and without a new product to hook us in they tell us it's both new and improved.

Even if they aren't lying, and it is both new and improved, new could simply mean a new label, and improved could mean that instead of tasting like dog excrement, it's now been upgraded to taste more like cat.

Advertising and marketing exists solely to create the idea that you are missing out, and without product X Y Z, life is simply not worth living. That's a really easy job when talking about things that conjure up emotions – things such as holidays or food. People can easily picture themselves lying on the beach or tucking into that tasty joint of roast beef.

It's not so easy when talking about kitchen tongs or garden furniture. In order to sell these products, they use things called shopping channels. If you are ever feeling a bit down-in-the-dumps, I urge you to watch twenty minutes of any given shopping channel. Suddenly life feels a little bit better. In my opinion shopping channels are second only to Jeremy Kyle when it comes to making you feeling better about yourself. Doctors should stop prescribing anti-depressants and start prescribing QVC or, in really bad cases, Bid Up TV.

The strange thing about shopping channels is that they actually seem to work. There are actually people not only watching these channels, but phoning in and buying the products. Some even have a little chat with the presenter. "That's right, Simon, I was just sitting here flicking through the channels thinking, if only I could get my hands on a set of purple feng shui cat ornaments!"

The frustrating thing about all of this is that while writing today's chapter, I haven't been able to truly concentrate on the job in hand. All I've been able to think about is why my stupid earphones are round and not ear-shaped.

Wednesday 17th October 2012

Today I decided to re-write this chapter. I had followed my usual morning routine and settled down in my usual seat and begun tapping away. It was an ok piece. It didn't really need re-writing.

This book and the chapters within are never pre-planned and the process of writing is an organic one. Things happen and then they get written about.

I received a call about half an hour ago from my mum. The call was expected, but it didn't make it any easier to deal with. My dear old gramps had passed away, two weeks after his 86th birthday. Without going into too much detail, he had been ill for a long time. In a previous chapter I talked about helping raise money for the McMillan nurses, for it was my gramps who was in their care. Gramps had always been an active man and continued to play bowls right up until his body decided he shouldn't anymore. Within months of giving up the bowls and driving the car, he began to lose his sight.

Gramps suffered from a rare condition that rendered him completely blind and it was this that frustrated him more than the lack of mobility. "At least I could live a normal life in a wheelchair", he would say. "I'd rather lose both my legs than both my eyes", he'd often proclaim. What upset him more than anything was that he would never see his newborn great-grandchildren. His memory was fading, but at least he had a vague picture of the older family members. With the new additions he couldn't, and babies don't take kindly to being poked and prodded by tobacco-stained fingers.

In the last year or so gramps had been struggling with stomach pains and, after a lot of persuasion, he visited the hospital, to be given the news that he had terminal bowel cancer. Gramps was well-known for being the pessimistic type, and when Victor Meldrew graced our screens in the early nineties even he could see the similarity. Given the awful news, gramps could have been forgiven for uttering Victor's famous line, but he didn't. He simply said "It is what it is and it will happen when it happens."

The last few months were tough for gramps, and in a way even tougher for my nan, who at

83 was having to do everything for him, even carrying him up and down the stairs. As a family we did all that we could, but we needed some extra help and that's where the McMillan nurses come in. I've never seen the nurses myself, but I've been told what a wonderful job they do. They remind me of the story of the elves and the shoemaker, where they sneak in unseen at the hour of need and sneak out again when it's time to say thank you.

Gramps was a simple man. Give him a roast dinner, a packet of chocolate brazils and a black and white film on the telly and he was a happy man. There was a longer list of things he didn't like than things he did. Loud music, cold food and drunk people were high on his list of dislikes, so parties with gramps were always a barrel of laughs.

Gramps was a proud man and loved talking about his adventures during the war. I'm really going to miss that. I was extremely lucky to have had him in my life and I hope that he is in a happy, comfortable, peaceful place right now.

I'm sorry for the lack of humour today, but I'm sure you understand in the circumstances.

It's a shame because the stuff I wrote this morning was bloody hilarious!

Dedicated to Albert Leeks, 03/10/1926 – 17/10/2012.

Friday 19th October 2012

Over the last couple of years our daughter has been suffering from various colds and viruses and, as a result, has always struggled to breath through her nose. It's a fairly minor thing, but it does disturb her sleep as it causes her to snore and it also affects her eating as she can only breathe through her mouth and her taste and smell are affected.

After many trips to the doctors she was referred to the hospital, and in late September we went to see an ENT specialist in Maidstone who confirmed that our daughter should have an adenoidectomy. After a puzzled look from me, the doctor confirmed that this was removal of the adenoids. A further puzzled look required the doctor to explain what the adenoids are and what they do.

Apparently they are small lumps of tissue, located above the tonsils, which help fight off infections and viruses. Hers have been overworked and they are now swollen and inflamed and unable to carry out their job. Her adenoids obviously felt overworked and undervalued and decided to go on strike. Only they haven't just gone on strike, they are actively making things worse. It would be like a fireman not only refusing to go to work, but going around town starting fires. Or like a soldier crossing enemy lines and opening fire upon his erstwhile comrades. What we are taking about here is a traitor. A Judas. Our daughter is having to deal with a traitor within. That's a lot for a three year-old to have to deal with.

The doctor explained that we should receive a letter confirming when the operation and the pre-operation assessment would take place.

"It could take up to three months", he said.

"Wow, I know Royal Mail are slow, but......"

"The date of the operation," the doctor interrupted, "Not the letter, the letter should be with you in the next week or so."

As promised, the letter arrived a week later; it confirmed that our daughter's operation was booked for the 29th October and her pre-operation assessment was to be on the 18th October. We were both impressed and delighted with the news. You see, three months would have meant our daughter having an operation near Christmas – not the best time for any child to be feeling under the weather, but as our daughter's birthday is on New Year's Eve, it really would have been a double whammy.

We were also happy because we were told by the doctor that she would need a week at home to recover during which she wasn't to go out, which meant that one of us would have to stay home. The 29th October is the first day of the school holidays and with my wife being a teacher it works out perfectly.

People complain about the NHS all the time and I'm sure often with good reason. It isn't perfect and I'm sure they get things wrong a lot of the time, but my issue with that is that you never hear about the times when they get it right. Today I am going to tell you about how they got it right.

Obviously, the first positive thing for us was the speed with which our daughter received her operation date. It could have taken three months, it took just one. Yesterday, we drove over to the hospital, a different one to where she had had the referral. It's a fairly new hospital and it was very impressive. There was ample parking, which for once had a sensible tariff. The first half an hour was free and then it went up in sensible amounts after that. Watford General Hospital (and yes, I am happy to name and shame them) have a ridiculous parking policy. They have a minimum charge of £4, so even if you are back within ten minutes, it will still cost you £4! Every three hours, it will cost you another £4. When our daughter was born there, I spent over £40 on parking.

The reception area of the hospital was also impressive. It was a large, open, welcoming space. There were about ten 'Check In' terminals, where you scan in the barcode of your letter and it confirms your arrival and lets you know where to go and wait. Within two minutes we were in a large waiting room which once again felt open, spacious and welcoming. There were plenty of toys for the children and reading materials for the adults. There were also two huge flat-screen monitors that would flash up a name every few seconds directing each patient to their consultation room. So far there has been no contact with a human. You might think this is bad, but I don't. You might think that back in the 'good old days' you would have been checked in by a receptionist, and beckoned into your room by a nurse, and that the introduction of a computerised system has rendered them jobless and on the scrapheap, but it hasn't. The receptionists and nurses are still there, it's just that now they can do other, more important tasks, such as writing up notes, filing reports and fetching test results.

The way I look at it is if a job can be done more efficiently by a computerised system, then go ahead and computerise it. Why settle for second best? The system that the hospital uses to check people in and send them to their consultation rooms is better than a human because it does a better job. It never calls in sick, it never needs a lunch break and it is never caught flirting with Dr Thomas. On top of all that it can speak over 200 languages. By employing a computerised system to check people in and move them around the hospital, they can spend money on other crucial employees that often get overlooked, like the porters and the cleaners. No computer system in the world is going to be able to move a bed from one ward to another or a rubbish bag from the ward to the incinerator.

I was hugely impressed with the whole operation. The staff seemed happy and well-organised and the patients looked comfortable and at ease. We were seen five minutes earlier than our appointment time – another advantage of a computerised system, as it can spot gaps and prioritise accordingly, dealing with hundreds of patients at a time. We were in and out in less than forty minutes and we even found time to visit the coffee shop situated within the hospital.

Our visit was completely stress-free, which was in stark contrast to the visit I made to another hospital on Tuesday evening to see my dear old gramps. It is really refreshing to see that new technology is not only being embraced, it's making a real difference.

Monday 22nd October 2012

This morning I have to make an admission. It's finally time for me to be honest and admit that I drink too much. This weekend was the worst I have been for a long time. I'm not sure whether it's the stress of bereavement, the stress of work or the general stress of family life, but I just couldn't seem to stop myself this weekend. Even more worrying was that I mixed my drinks. I got to the stage where it didn't matter what it was, so long as it was coffee.

That's right, coffee. Over the course of one weekend I managed to drink about fifteen cups of coffee in various forms, whether it be instant, filter, americano or latte. I even had a slice of coffee cake!

Ever since I gave up alcohol, nearly three years ago, I have become a coffee freak. I seem to crave coffee more than I ever did alcohol. I've given up one drug and replaced it with another.

I gave up drinking by accident. I never intended to give up. I went to the doctor's one day with a relatively minor ailment that needed treating with antibiotics. In order for the antibiotics to work I had to make sure that I didn't drink any alcohol for seven days. Seven days might not sound a lot, but for me back then it was. I used to drink regularly, and by that I mean most days. I always seemed to have a reason; sometimes I would find a reason to celebrate; sometimes it was a bad day at work; sometimes it was simply a stressful commute. Strange, isn't it, that alcohol can treat so many moods?

I never considered myself to be an alcoholic. Alcoholics roamed parks and congregated on park benches; they didn't have a job and have a cheeky few after work.

When I think about it now, I realise that I did have a drink problem. Whenever I met up with friends I would arrive early and have a couple of drinks before they arrived, sometimes I would even have a couple at home before going out. Suddenly, instead of having a few beers at the football with my friends, I started to watch it on the telly at home with only the beer to keep me company. Soon I had moved from having a glass of wine with dinner to having a few glasses, and the quick beer after work turned into a few. It wasn't long before every day seemed to be a 'stressful day'.

Looking back now, I was an alcoholic, pure and simple. There tend to be three accepted 'stages' or 'forms' of alcoholism, depending on which information you read. They are hazardous, harmful and dependant. I would say that I was firmly in the dependant stage, slowly working my way towards harmful. No, I didn't swig from brown paper bags, I didn't ever drink during the day, but I did get to the point where a drink was the only thing that could relax me after a hard day.

It was quite hard for me to write that last sentence, but it's easy for me to write the next one. Giving up alcohol was best thing I ever did. If I was being dramatic, or maybe if I was American, I would probably say it saved my life.

So, the doctor told me I needed to take some tablets and I wasn't allowed to drink alcohol for a week. A week later and my ailment was treated, my blood pressure had gone down and I had lost nine pounds in weight. (Four kilos in new money.)

Bloody hell! Those tablets must have been good!

I knew then that while the tablets may have helped, it was the absence of alcohol that had really made the difference. I actually think that the ailment itself was a warning mechanism within me to get me to the doctor, like the warning light on a car. It was time for this old banger to see the mechanic.

So many people get that warning light, but how many people do anything about it? Here is a question for you. What is the best way of dealing with the warning light in a car?

Is it:

A) Find out what the problem is and fix it. The mechanic confirms that it's the oil light, so you give him the go-ahead to top up the oil.

Or is it:

B) Who knows what it is? Let's just unscrew the bulb. No more warning light, no more problem!

As you probably know, solution A will result in a healthy car, solution B will result in a trip to the scrap-yard. I honestly believe that there are hundreds of thousands, if not millions, of people who are happily selecting option B and unscrewing the bulb when it comes to their health. Doctors and patients alike are happy to treat the effect, flagrantly ignoring the cause.

You might be expecting me to say that giving up alcohol was hard, but it wasn't. It was easy. The easiest thing I have ever done. I didn't go cold turkey; I didn't spend months in a dark room craving alcohol; I didn't go to any meetings; I didn't feel sorry for myself. I simply used the most powerful tool available to me.

I used my brain.

It may sound simplistic, but I simply told myself that I didn't need to drink any more. Cravings are easy to deal with if you know how. Every time I had a craving for alcohol, I turned that negative, sad and empty feeling into a positive, happy and fulfilled feeling. Instead of feeling sad that I no longer drank alcohol, I was able to flip that emotion on its head, immediately feeling happy that I didn't.

It's very similar to how you would think about your ex-boyfriend or girlfriend, the one that cheated on you. I'm sure that when things were going well, you couldn't get enough of them, and every time you thought about them you had that warm, happy and contented feeling. Skip forward, six months later, to when you found out that they had cheated on you with your best friend. I'm sure very different emotions surface, such as sadness, anger and hatred. It's the same memory, you are just able to attach a different emotion.

My visit to the doctor not only confirmed that alcohol had cheated on me with my best friend, it confirmed that it had been controlling my life and was now threatening to kill me.

Some friend alcohol turned out to be.

My new friend coffee treats me much better but there are times, like at three o'clock this morning, where I lie there, wide awake, thinking to myself "Why did coffee have to become my new friend?"

Tuesday 23rd October 2012

I've been asked to write the eulogy for my gramps. I'd already decided that I wanted to, and I was really glad when my nan said that she'd like me to do it.

I'm extremely proud to be doing it, but there's also a lot of pressure. Chiefly there's the pressure of writing it. I've got to sum up my gramps' life in about five minutes. The bits about his childhood in the East End of London and the bit about joining the army and fighting in World War II take up fifteen minutes alone. I've decided that I'm going to speak about gramps from a grandchild's perspective. I'm going to talk about all of the things we used to enjoy doing with him, and all of the happy memories that I have of that time. I've decided that the best way to sum this up is in a poem.

I'm not sure if this is a sensible decision. I've tried writing poetry many times before. Firstly, with catastrophic results, as a 10 year-old schoolboy. One of my first crushes was on a girl called Sonja. Yes, that's how she spelled it. I liked Sonja, but Sonja didn't like me. She was very good friends with Laura and, to complicate matters, Laura had a crush on me, but of course I didn't have a crush on her. We had this weird triangle where Laura had a crush on me, I had a crush on Sonja, and Sonja had a crush on neither of us. It was not so much a love-triangle, more of a love-cul-de-sac.

It was going nowhere, so I decided that poetry was the best way forward. I can't remember exactly what I wrote, but it was around the theme of 'Roses are Red; Violets are Blue', as it was popular at the time. The boys used to shout it out in class towards the girls they disliked, with the finishing lines inevitably being something like "I hate you 'coz you smell of poo!"

I was sure I had written a poetic masterpiece. I was sure it was going to win Sonja over. My only issue was how to get it to Sonja. I decided that the best person to deliver this masterpiece was Laura.

Big mistake.

Laura kept her promise. She delivered my masterpiece, only she didn't just deliver it to Sonja, she delivered it, out loud, to the whole class. I was mortified. It took weeks to get over, and it was years before I would write any poetry again.

I've decided I need to practice. If I am going to write the eulogy in the form of a poem, I need some practice at writing poems first. I've decided that the best platform is this book. I have a book to write and I have a eulogy to write, so why not combine both?

It's far too late to change the past; there's nothing I could do

It all just seemed to change so fast; trouble seemed to brew

I hadn't felt his lips for weeks, that's just how it started

I felt just like an old antique, shattered, broken hearted

A newer model appeared one day, tall and sleek from China

What was wrong, he didn't say, the details seemed so finer

Washed up thoughts fade to black, he left me out to dry

Even when I began to crack, I never thought I'd cry

He picked me up; he put me down, tears a little closer

The final, awful, painful sound, her settling on his coaster

So that's my story, time is up; I really need a hug

Now he's got his china cup, he doesn't need a mug.

I'm not sure that it's up to the standard of the poem I wrote for Sonja, but I enjoyed writing it and it's given me the confidence to write the eulogy now. The only thing I am worried about now is delivering it.

I'm a confident guy, and talking to large groups of people does not worry me, but talking to large groups of people while crying and wiping away snot does. There will be people who are upset, myself included, and the most important thing for me is to try to hold it together. I've been able to practise writing the poem, but I won't be able to practise reading it. Sure, I can read it in front of a mirror a thousand times, but I will never be able to replicate the day itself. I just hope I can hold it together.

The last thing I want is for someone else to read out one of my poems again.

Wednesday 24th October 2012

Dreams are strange, aren't they? Last night I decided to watch two programmes, back-to-back, all about the vile man that was Jimmy Savile. The true extent of this man's evil is yet to be fully uncovered, but I would hope that the whole truth will be available by the time this book is printed. The two programmes had been recorded from the previous night.

There was a Newsnight programme, hosted by Jeremy Paxman, which essentially slated the editor of the programme and then proceeded to interview the programme's own journalists, reaffirming the point that Newsnight's editor was an idiot. It was a Newsnight special, about Newsnight; very strange indeed. It would be like a private investigator hiring himself to investigate his own private life.

The second programme was Panorama, which also focused on the same issues, but went into more detail about Savile himself and how he could have possibly got away with it for so long. It finished by questioning whether senior bosses at the BBC, including the director general, were involved in a cover up. Two BBC programmes, aired at the same time, one on

BBC 1, the other on BBC 2, both primarily concerned with criticising the BBC.

Whatever you think about the BBC, you have got to admire their balls.

So having watched both of these programmes back-to-back, relatively late last night, I inevitably started to dream about it. Last night I became the lead investigator in the case and it was down to me to get to the truth. I spent the whole night conducting interviews with BBC staff, including journalists, presenters, editors, producers and even the bloody security guard on the gate. I interviewed victims, witnesses, family members; I held press conferences, spoke to MPs and even took advice from the queen. This morning I am exhausted.

I'd like to say that I cracked the case, but of course I didn't. While interviewing the staff at the BBC, the office I was in suddenly became a circus tent, the person I was speaking to suddenly turned into an orange, and the paper I was writing on turned into a paper plane and flew away.

One minute I was interviewing the director general at BBC headquarters, the next I was interviewing a bloody orange in a circus tent. In truth, it really hindered my investigation, but, as always in dreams, I never questioned it for a second. I was determined to get to the truth and if it had to come from a tangerine, then so be it.

Of course, like all dreams, it was just a jumbled-up mess and none of it made any sense. I still woke up, tired and confused, convinced that I'd made some inroads and some of the leads were worth following up. I often have the dream where I've won the lottery and I'm convinced that I'll be able to recall at least some of the numbers.

"I'm sure there was a six... Or was it a nine? I remember the number one... Or was it eleven...?"

The worst dream is the one about work. I have a recurring dream where I spend the whole night dreaming about work. Tossing and turning all night long, work work work, only to wake up and have to do it all again, only for bloody real. Twenty four hours of non-stop bloody work. So unfair.

The other dream I have regularly is the one where I'm convinced I can remember it all, but can in fact remember nothing. I'll say to my wife:

"I had a dream about us last night where we were in Paris."

"Really? What happened?" she'll ask.

"Well you were there, only it wasn't you, it was someone else... And we went to Paris, only it wasn't Paris, it was somewhere else..."

Twenty minutes later and I am still trying to explain the 'vivid' dream that I had, with the only recalled details being that my wife was there but she wasn't, and we went to Paris but we didn't.

Popular dreams tend to focus on fantasy, so guys will often dream about playing up-front for their favourite football team, and girls will often dream about being a princess and marrying a prince. I've always wondered what footballers and princesses dream about. Maybe they dream about driving a van or working in a shop.

Dreams offer an alternative reality, and I think they're a good thing, even if that means I have to wake up every so often wondering why my doctor is the new Prime Minister.

As Gabrielle once famously sang, "Dreams can come true", so if you'll excuse me, I have some crucial leads to follow up on.

Tuesday 30th October 2012

You may have noticed that it has been six days since my last chapter. Unfortunately I had to attend my gramps' funeral on Friday and yesterday I had to spend the day in hospital. When I originally booked the Friday and Monday off, a colleague in HR asked if I was up to anything nice.

"Funeral on the Friday, day in hospital looking after my ill daughter on the Monday." I replied.

"Oh," she said. "Enjoy!"

Enjoy?

To be honest, I'm not sure what I would have said if I was put in that same situation. Good luck is about the only response which fits both occasions, although I've never liked wishing people luck. It's essentially saying "Look buddy, you're on your own. I can't help you and neither can anyone else, the only thing that will get you through this is a massive stroke of luck."

There are times when it's right to wish someone good luck. If someone enters a raffle, go ahead and wish them luck. Everybody has the same chance (assuming everyone has just one ticket, let's not get technical here). If someone enters the X Factor it wouldn't be right to wish them luck, as luck has nothing to do with it. It would be down to their talent and how strong their sob-story was, nothing to do with luck at all. You should simply say "I hope you sing well", or "I hope you manage to cry in all the close-ups".

When someone goes for a job interview the stock response is "good luck", but again, luck has nothing to do with it. You should simply say "I hope you give interesting and insightful answers and that you are able to accurately communicate your ability to work independently or as part of a team." Or if you were being especially honest, you would say "I hope you don't bore them to death with your stories of how misunderstood you are, how unlucky in love you are and why you can't understand why no-one else has been willing to offer you a job."

Anyway, I can honestly say, even though the two events were separated by a weekend, I still feel absolutely shattered. I feel both emotionally and physically exhausted. On Friday I had to say goodbye to my gramps and I was honoured when I was asked to do the eulogy. I always thought that I'd be preparing a best man speech way before being asked to prepare a eulogy, but life is rarely straightforward. I managed to write a poem that summed up my gramps and I delivered it with what I would describe as 'controlled emotion'.

There were pauses, and at times my voice cracked and wobbled. At one point I produced a noise that I am unfamiliar with, and I think only dogs would be able to decipher, but I managed to compose myself and finish the poem. Many people came up to me afterwards and said how nice the poem was, and one person said that having watched what I did they would be changing their funeral plans and would be asking one of their grandchildren to do the same.

Poor bastards! I really feel for them!

Wednesday 31st October 2012

Today is Halloween and, with it falling on a Wednesday, I have had to put up with seeing photos of fully grown adults dressed up as ghosts, goblins and mummies since last Friday. As it has fallen mid-week, I will have to put up with it right up until this Sunday. Nine days of watching adults behave like children. I've never had anything against Halloween but it does frustrate me that it is annoyingly close to Bonfire Night.

It's like Christmas and New Year. Two celebrations that are annoyingly close. Ok, it works well in the sense that we get an extended Christmas break, but then we have to wait another three or four months until Easter arrives.

We should move a couple of our celebration days so that they are sensibly spaced out throughout the year. Christmas should stay where it is, because it makes sense that it should be cold at Christmas. Reindeers work well in the cold, Santa is always suitably dressed, and who wants to eat a Christmas pudding in August?

Easter should stay in where it is too. We should move Halloween to June, have the New Year in August and Bonfire Night should stay where it is in November. By doing this, there is a suitable gap between all of the celebrations and people can enjoy each one on its own merit.

Halloween in June would have its challenges, but none that could not be overcome. It's lighter in the evenings for a start, so although it wouldn't have the same spooky feel, children would inevitably be safer. Pumpkins are not ready for harvest in June, so people would have to be a little more creative, but I think that's a good thing – people have been far too lazy for far too long. Let's see what people can create from onions, broad beans, beetroot, cabbage, asparagus and strawberries. I can already picture far more intricate vegetable-based doorstep lanterns.

Having the New Year in August also makes perfect sense. Ok, there's some work to do on the calendar side of things, but it's a lovely month to go out and celebrate something. My birthday's in August and I can vouch for it being a good party month. It's well before

Christmas, so money will be less of an issue, and it's relatively warm, so you wouldn't have to worry about getting frostbite when you decided to walk home because there were no taxis.

Now, going back to the calendar, it would seem a bit weird to have the New Year on the 31st August, so we would probably have to rename the months. So August would now be called December, September would be January, and so on.

This would cause a lot of confusion, I agree, but it would all be worth it in the end. So, Christmas would be on 25th April, (but it would still be cold, don't worry;) Easter, confusingly, would be in July, because although it is normally in April, next year it falls at the end of March, so with my new calendar it would fall in July and not August. To really confuse matters, even though I've just moved Halloween to June, with my new calendar, Halloween would now be back in October. Of course, we'd have the added complication of the Winter as we know it becoming Spring, the Spring becoming Summer, Summer becoming Autumn and Autumn becoming Winter, so I've decided to summarise things below.

31st December (New Year's Eve) – I've moved the date to 31st August, but then moved the calendar so that it still falls at the end of December.

5th March (Bonfire Night) – I've kept the date the same, the dates have just changed due to the calendar shift.

25th April (Christmas Day) – Same as above.

29th July (Good Friday) – Same as above, but of course the Easter dates change every year.

31st October (Halloween) – I've moved the date to the 30th June (as June only has 30 days, not 31,) but then moved the calendar, which means that June has become October again, so I've moved the date back to the 31st.

Why this simple solution has not been put forward before, I will never know!

Friday 2nd November 2012

This morning I feel like a teenager again. I don't mean it in the same way as when middle-aged people say it to try to explain how they feel when they finally meet someone who wants to have sex with them. No, I feel like a teenager again because I have woken up with a massive spot on my nose.

I feel that I need to explain exactly how big this spot is. You are probably picturing a red mark, a relatively small, insignificant mark that any adult could easily get on with. Stop picturing that small red mark. This is not a small red mark. This is not a spot, a blemish or a pimple. This is a huge embarrassing zit.

It's so big that it seems to have its own pulse. It's in that awkward place where I can actually see it out of the corner of my eye. I can't even just try to forget about it, as every time I look down I think I've smeared jam on my face.

I would honestly rather have a black eye or a busted nose than have to deal with this spot. I would rather people assume that I have a drink problem or that I am the victim of domestic abuse than have them looking at my spot and questioning my facial hygiene.

When I think about it, I probably have neglected my face when it comes to pampering. I watch my wife do things to her face that I thought were only carried out at spas. When I say spas, I mean the things that used to be called health-farms before fat people started going, not the chain of tired old convenience-stores where fat people have always been going.

I've been reliably informed in the past that my wife washes, tones, cleanses and moisturises, although I will never know in which order they happen. If she were a car, she would be selecting the Platinum Wash and if I were a car, I would simply be using a bucket and sponge, probably bought from Spa.

As a man in his thirties, I feel woefully exposed, without any excuses to cling to or make-up to hide behind. If I were a teenager, or for that matter a woman, it could easily be excused as something to do with hormones, diet or stress, or a combination of all three; but I'm not – I'm a balding bloke in his thirties.

I've decided that I'm going to have to try to cover it up; it is just too big to ignore. If I left it, it wouldn't just be the elephant in the room, it would be the mammoth in the broom-cupboard. People would be talking to me, thinking "Don't mention the zit", and I would be thinking "He's noticed the zit and now I've put him in the awkward position of having to tell himself not to mention the zit".

As soon as this train pulls in to the station I'm going to make my way to Boots to buy some plasters. I will select the smallest one and place it over the bridge of my nose. There are three ways to play this.

Option 1. Stroll confidently into work, plaster on nose, and say nothing. A risky strategy which will almost certainly result in whispers and strange looks, but I might just be able to get through the day unscathed.

Option 2. Stroll confidently into work, plaster on nose, and say that they were not wrong about these nasal breathing strips – that was the best night's sleep I've had in ages. Another risky strategy, as I might have to explain the pros and cons of a product that I have neither used, nor intend to use.

Option 3. Stroll confidently into work, plaster on nose, and say "Look everyone, I have a huge spot on my nose, and I can't face you having to look at this disgusting scab on my face all day, so I've done the best I could in a bad situation. It's covered up, I know it looks stupid, but can we all just get on with the day? I'll make the coffee, and let's all just concentrate on the fact that it's the weekend in nine hours' time."

Against my better judgment, I'm going to go for option three. I'll be completely honest about why it's there, while not brave enough to actually show why it's there.

Honesty over bravery. The wimp's way out.

Never take me to war; the enemy would have me blurting out secrets before they had a chance to strap me to the chair.

Monday 5th November 2012

This morning I spent ten minutes searching for some old work-trousers. This happens from time to time when I realise that my preferred pairs are either in the wash or still scrunched up on the floor behind the wash basket.

Today it happened for a different reason.

Today it happened because I can no longer fit into them. I have two pairs of trousers in my current waist size which I alternate. Suddenly, neither pair fit me. How can that happen? One weekend of careless eating and suddenly it's impossible to do either pair up. Surely they must have shrunk in the wash. Surely someone is playing a practical joke and altering my clothes in my sleep. Surely someone has switched them for another size. Surely!

Looking back, the warning signs have been there for a while. Last week I was forced to change my penny/split ratio. This is a complex ratio between the value of coin that I am prepared to pick up, compared to the potential risk of my trousers splitting. It's always hovered around 5 pence, but I've recently had to increase it to 20. I've also found myself emptying my pockets before I sit down. Sitting down with a phone and keys in my pocket will either result in the items being buried so deeply into my legs it would take four of the country's most gifted surgeons fourteen hours to remove, or, depending on the fabric, the trousers will simply explode under the pressure. An office full of men in tight trousers with full pockets could easily turn into a warzone as buttons fly across the office and shrapnel-like wounds are created by the trousers that have held fast. If you ever see a man emptying his pockets before sitting down, it's not because he needs to use his mobile, it's because he's deeply worried about the onset of this chaos.

I have to be honest and admit that it has not just been one weekend of careless eating; it has been many weekends combined with many weekdays too. I've slowly been putting on weight for the last couple of months and unlike most people, who like to blame stress or glands, I simply need to blame myself. You see, in my case it's rebound. I lost almost six stone two years ago. (That's 84 pounds to any Americans reading and 38 kilos to everyone else. Why we Brits continue to weigh in stones, I will never know!)

How did I do it? Very simple indeed. I started eating the right food in the right quantities at the right times. I also started exercising more. That's it. There isn't any secret formula, you simply need to want to do it in the first place and then have the mental strength to carry it out. I cut down my portion sizes, cut out all of the unnecessary snacks and started to walk everywhere. I didn't go on any fancy diet that involved me counting points or having red or green days, I simply questioned what went in my mouth every time I ate. If I really wanted something, I had it. It's about moderation, and trusting yourself to make the right choices. I never felt unhappy or deprived while using this self-taught method of losing weight. If you make your goal achievable and hold it in high-enough regard, then I'm certain this method will work perfectly for anyone.

So what went wrong? I started to ignore the rules! I was still questioning what I ate, so the alarm system was still functioning perfectly, but my inner security guard seemed intent on ignoring the alarm-bells, the guard-dogs, the searchlights and even the bloody CCTV. Every time I ate something bad, the alarm would ring, the dogs would bark, the searchlight would kick in and the CCTV would be filming the crime taking place, but the security guard would just shrug, turn the page of his book and take another bite of his pizza.

When I was losing weight, the single most satisfying thing about the whole process was purchasing new clothes. Now I'm putting some weight back on, I realise that the single most depressing thing is having to rummage through the cupboard and pull out the saggy old discarded clothes from before.

So today I'm going to recruit a new security guard. One who cares. One who jumps to his feet even before the dog starts barking. One who patrols the perimeter gate. One who's armed with a truncheon and not afraid to use it.

This book was born from a self-imposed challenge and now I am going to use it to set myself another. I'm going to set myself the challenge of losing twenty pounds by the 14th December. That's just over nine kilos in just under six weeks. Twenty pounds, as that is how much weight I have put on, and the 14th December as that is the date that the first part of this book will be released.

I've always set myself challenges and, while I've not always succeeded, I've always given it my best. If I don't succeed this time, I'll be completely honest, and I'll know exactly whom to blame. That lazy, bone-headed, good-for-nothing security guard.

Tuesday 6th November 2012

While standing in the queue at a mini-supermarket yesterday lunchtime, I noticed that they had hidden all of their tobacco products behind a sliding door, and the notice on the front of it read something like "If you are buying tobacco products please let a member of staff know and we will assist you".

I knew that there was a rule coming into place meaning this step had to be taken, but wasn't aware that it had come into force, as I normally do my food shopping online. Apparently, according to ex-health minister Anne Milton, "Banning these displays will help young people resist the pressure to start smoking and help thousands of adults in England who are currently trying to quit".

Really? The law only requires shops of a certain size to take this step, so the only establishments currently obeying this ludicrous rule are supermarkets. How many children pop into the supermarket on their way home from school? How many children ignore the corner-shop in favour of the out-of-town supermarket?

Let's look at the second part of that statement – "help thousands of adults in England who are currently trying to quit". How will this help the thousands who are trying to quit? How is hiding tobacco products in supermarkets going to truly help anyone addicted to nicotine? If anyone happened to be struggling with nicotine addiction and needed a quick fix, I doubt they would jump in their car and head to the nearest supermarket; they would almost certainly do what anyone would do with any addiction, and go to the nearest possible place to get their fix. That place is the same place that children get their sweets – the local shop.

Even if they did, do you really think that once they got to the supermarket and failed to find the tobacco products, they would just give up and say "Oh well, looks like they've sold out, silly me, what a fool I've been, let that be a lesson to me"? No, they would do what any of us would do in the same situation, and ask someone. Instead of a spotty fourteen year-old having to explain to an octogenarian why they have moved the tinfoil to the crisp aisle, you now have the situation where a spotty fourteen year-old is having to explain to a grown adult that they have in fact hidden them, and for their own good.

In order for this stupid law to have any hope of working, it needs to be employed by everyone. That's not going to happen, and rightly so; why should shopkeepers throughout the country have to bear such a huge cost to undertake such a stupid idea? I don't know the solution, but I do know that hiding products from view in a small percentage of outlets is a stupid idea. It would be like telling the supermarkets to cordon off their cakes, and then releasing a statement saying "Look, we're helping fatties to get thinner!"

As I stood in the supermarket queue, it wasn't just the sliding door covering the tobacco products that annoyed me; the automatic queue-caller annoyed me too. I don't know what else to call it, but it's that annoying voice that says "Till number 3 is now available". Its monotone, featureless, automaton voice was already quite high on the "What could be the most annoying sound in the universe?" scale, but then it suddenly started switching voices, alternating between male and female.

"Ah, but we don't want to come across as sexist", someone in a suit presumably thought. And no, you don't come across as sexist, you just come across as stupid. Even worse than that, in your desperate attempt to come across as all politically correct, you in fact seem to have assumed that your customers are all stupid. Without the inclusion of both a male and female voice, you seem to think that we will be marching down equality street, pitchforks in hand, headed for the equality street police station. It's a bloody recorded voice. It can be male or female, and no-one would care either way. Chill out, Mr PC, and take a look at the other parts of your store which actually do need looking at.

Instead of adding to the obesity epidemic, why don't you stop offering "Buy one get one free", and start offering 50% off like you used to, before you started messing around with robot voices. Why don't you look at the fact that your fruit and veg has an even bigger carbon footprint than your vastly overpaid managing director. Why don't you stop trying to pull the wool over our eyes by claiming that products are "Tasty" and "Nutritious" when they are about as tasty and nutritious as a turd dipped in chocolate.

As much as I hate shopping online, at least I don't have to put up with hermaphrodite robots and pointless games of hide-and-seek.

Wednesday 7th November 2012

It annoys me that I have to shave. My hair stopped growing some time ago now, and only requires a token trim around the back and sides every few months. If I'm totally honest, that particular cut, which I carry out by myself, is more of an excuse to keep the neck and ear hair under control than it is to keep any actual head hair in check. My face has no such problems; in fact, since the hair stopped growing on my head, my face seems to have taken on the extra responsibility by growing hair faster than ever before.

My head and face is like a village with two bakers, both of them happily going about their business, neither of them overworked, both happily making a living, until suddenly baker number one, let's call him Mr Baker, dies. Now baker number two, let's not call him Mr Baker, let's just call him Bob, is left inundated, having to serve the whole of the village. Bob (my face) has taken it upon himself, out of respect for Mr Baker (my head hair), to bridge the gap and serve the whole of the village (grow more hair). That is possibly the most stupid analogy I have ever come up with, but I like referring to my stubble as Bob and my bald head as Mr Baker, so it's staying.

I found out to my horror a few years ago that as you get older, the hair that you want to grow doesn't and the hair that you don't want to grow does. It's a weird thing the body decides to do as you advance in years. I see it as a punishment for getting older and therefore having less to worry about. I've long since stopped worrying about females, friends and fashion, so my body's replaced that with worries about ear, nose and back hair. Thank you, body, thank you very much.

Hair in general has many functions, but the hair on your head is there primarily for warmth and protection. Surely then, when you get to the time of your life where you spend half of your time buying blankets and the other half falling over, you should be growing more hair on your head, not less? I reckon that if it weren't for flat caps the average life-expectancy for a man would be somewhere around 55.

Tuesday 13th November 2012

My wife and I have a fairly good system. I take care of the finances, the cooking and the food-shopping, and she takes care of the cleaning, washing and diary-management. Both of us know our roles, so it's very rare that we argue over who should do what. Obviously there are cross-over points where there is too much work for one, so if we are hosting a dinner party my wife will put on her apron, and if there's a spring-clean to be done I'll ask my mother-in-law round for coffee.

I have to admit that I have it fairly easy. Looking after the finances is an easy-enough job because that's what I do for a day job, and the cooking provides enjoyment and relaxation from the stresses of commuting and working in London. This weekend we had the in-laws round, and I decided to do a couple of courses. The weather has turned very cold and wet, so I thought I'd go for two winter favourites: soup followed by a roast. What had seemed a fairly simple meal actually turned into a whole weekend of cooking, which went as follows:

The soup that I settled on was pea and ham, and I decided to cook it on Saturday, meaning we could enjoy it for lunch on Saturday and then have it for starters on Sunday too.

As I wasn't following a recipe, I had no idea how many peas to buy, so I bought a couple of kilos. Similarly, I had no idea how much ham to buy, so I asked the butcher if I could have some cooked ham that would go well in a pea and ham soup, and he sold me the end piece from a huge joint of ham.

"How about this piece?" he asked as he held it up.

"Perfect." I said, as I weighted up in my mind whether I actually needed that much ham and how much such a big piece would cost.

"That'll be a pound." he said.

I was astonished. One pound for what was clearly more than a pound (in weight) of prime pork. At first I thought that maybe he had given me a special deal because I had already spent £15 on a joint of pork but, having thought about it more, I think he is actually just a good businessman. If he had said £4 or £5, I might have said "No that's fine, I don't need the whole piece." He then would have been left with a piece of ham which would have been very difficult to sell, and he might even have ended up having to throw it away. I imagine one of the most frustrating things about being a retailer is throwing things away.

Retailers who sell fresh goods must hate throwing away stock that doesn't sell. Someone who runs a toy shop can simply run a sale of their old stock. There is no time frame as to when it needs to be sold by, and they would certainly not have to throw away any of their stock. Selling food must be extremely stressful as every fresh item is effectively a ticking time-bomb.

I made a decent job of the pea and ham soup, but I had enough to feed the whole village. The plan was to make it on Saturday so that we could have it for lunch, but there was enough to have it for breakfast, lunch and dinner for a whole week. It didn't go to waste, however, as we had it on Saturday and Sunday and our neighbours came round to have some too.

After making the soup I was left with some beautiful vegetable stock and, having learnt from the butcher, I decided not to throw it away. After racking my brain and raiding the cupboard, I decided on a risotto and set about whipping it up for our evening meal on Saturday.

On Sunday we had to be out by ten o'clock, because we were walking into the village to watch the remembrance service and pay our respects to soldiers past and present, so it meant starting on dinner at nine o'clock in the morning. Rather than doing a traditional roast I had decided to do 'pulled pork', which requires the pork to be slow-roasted for five to six hours. Once back from the service I set about preparing the potatoes and vegetables, while also reheating the soup. Lunch was a success, but once again there were plenty of leftovers. I decided that with so much pork left over, I had to make some apple sauce, so that we could enjoy a pork roll in the evening and also for sandwiches the following day.

The total time that I spent in the kitchen this weekend was twelve hours, but I'm not complaining, as I know I still have it easy when it comes to the household chores. That message was hammered home at around nice o'clock last night as I watched my wife sort through the washing basket, picking through my dirty pants, one by one.

Wednesday 14th November 2012

Today it was announced that there's a car being made by a French manufacturer which can be driven at the age of 16. It has a 400cc diesel engine, has a top speed of 28 mph, and weighs less than 350 kg. Due to these vehicular vital statistics it qualifies as a 'light quadricycle', but that is the only thing that can be described as light, as it will cost around £10,000 and likely cost any 16 year-old around £2,200 per year in tax.

A statement from the manufacturer said "We believe that the young rider market for scooters and mopeds has been contracting lately". Yes, because no-one can even afford a scooter these days, let alone a £10,000 quadricycle. They back up their point by saying that "This is due to the difficulty in convincing parents of the safety issues surrounding mopeds and scooters. This will offer a safer method of transport".

I don't think it's issues of safety stopping parents allowing their 16 year-old ASBO-owners to ride these death-machines, I think it's more to do with the fact that in the current financial climate, the parents of these children are finding that their benefits don't stretch as far anymore. These poor parents can barely afford their Rothmans and Carling, and they've had to tell their drug-dealer to only pop round once every fortnight, so something had to give. It isn't just sales of mopeds and scooters that are in decline though. What about Reebok Classics, string vests and pitbulls? Spare a thought if you will for establishments such as McDonald's, Sports Direct and Elizabeth Duke.

Those parents who do have the disposable income to afford such a car, and the insurance that goes with it, would simply not consider buying it. Precious Peter would be picked up by mummy, or perhaps Tarquin's mummy. This would carry on until Peter or Tarquin were old enough to drive their own proper car, at which point they would each buy a Citroen Saxo, spray-paint it lime-green, lower it, put a bass box in the boot and race it up and down Southend sea-front.

So who will buy a £10,000 quadricycle? There are people out there who buy another type of scooter, sales of which are most definitely on the up. Ladies and gentlemen, I give you the mobility-scooter. About ten years ago, the only people allowed on our pavements on four wheels were the disabled. Since then we have had an influx of mobility-scooters, carrying a range of elderly and obese people. These people don't need insurance, a licence or even a brain – they can simply spend £300 at Fatties R Us and go about causing misery for all who come into contact with them. There seem to be two types of mobility-scooter: ones that don't have any brakes and cause the person in charge of them to be rendered both blind and stupid, and ones that have a top speed of 2mph and cannot negotiate a gradient of more than 2%.

I would make it the law that all mobility-scooter users had to buy one of these new cars instead (and I am not including disabled people here, because they ride their motorised wheelchairs perfectly capably). Some might say that the danger would just be moved from the pavements to the roads, but I think it's a risk worth taking. All they ever seem to do is go to the shops and back, either to draw out their pension or buy chicken nuggets, so the total mileage would be negligible, meaning the actual risk to others on the road would be minimal.

Just close your eyes and imagine a pavement you can walk along, without fear of having your ankle crushed, or your toes squashed. We all know that the NHS is constantly struggling with their budgets and trying to find a way of cutting costs. Just think how much they would save in minor injuries admissions.

Friday 16th November 2012

We have the auditors in at work at the moment, and it's always a very strange time to be around the place. There are a team of people sitting in a small side-office going through all of our work in minute detail. It's like being back at school, waiting for your teacher to return your homework, only you can actually see them marking it, via the wonders of flexi-glass.

I remember one time at school when I had done a pretty good job on a Geography assignment and was looking forward to handing it in. Geography was one of my favourite subjects and, although I wasn't top of the class, I was in the top set and got on really well with the teacher. The lesson was in the afternoon, and Amit Patel came up to me and asked if I had completed the assignment and I said that I had. He asked if he could check mine over as he was unhappy with his and wanted to see what I had come up with, in order to get some ideas. Those weren't his exact words, but I imagine that's pretty much how it went down.

Amit was a star pupil; he had moved to the UK from Kenya the previous year and had gone straight into the top set for every subject. He was well-spoken, had rich relatives and was a bloody good cricketer to boot. In fact, he was so good that he became captain straight away, and in his second game for us got into the local papers for scoring 100 runs in a 20-over match; pretty good going for a 14 year-old.

Needless to say I was extremely proud and somewhat honoured when he asked to check my assignment for ideas and inspiration, so I gave it to him without a moment's hesitation. It seems that he was so inspired by my work that he decided to copy it, word for word.

Now the problem with copying homework is that, in order for it to work, you need to be clever in how you copy. I should know – I was an A-grade student when it came to copying. Essentially you copy the theme but change words and sentence structures. If there's an example, use a similar one, but make sure it's slightly different. I always made sure I wrote the last sentence myself and summarised it in my own way, often coming up with a different conclusion. This works in everything but Maths. Do that in Maths and you'll be advanced to the bottom set quicker than you can say "Amit Patel is a bastard".

Amit did a stupid thing by copying me word-for-word, but he was clever at the same time. He had worked out that he didn't need to change anything because he was regarded as cleverer than me, so when two identical pieces landed on the teacher's desk, it was me that was going to carry the can. That's exactly how it played out. Mrs Brambley, in big red biro, had written:

"Andrew, you have copied this word-for-word from Amit Patel. This is not acceptable. See me after class."

Amit ended up with an A-, and I ended up with a detention. The most frustrating thing about the whole thing is that he never admitted it. To this day that assignment was written by Amit Patel, and Mrs Brambley thinks I am a cheat. Still, he did get bowled for a duck in the next match we played together, so every cloud...

Anyway, auditors are generally very nice people and they do a very important job. Why is it then that I feel compelled to poison their coffee every time they say yes to a hot drink? They're just so bloody pedantic. Every single statistic, report and spreadsheet is checked in minute detail. They will come up to you with questions on things that you did eleven months ago. I often forget what I did eleven minutes ago, so eleven months is a real challenge. The only way around it is to do it again and provide them with a detailed run-through of how you got to where you did. Can you imagine doing that in any other occupation? Imagine asking a lorry-driver how many traffic lights he went through on his journey from Sheffield to Hull on the 10th December 2011, and then asking him to take the journey again when he couldn't come up with the answer.

I've come to the conclusion that auditors are the brainy cousins of personal trainers. They exist for the greater good, and the end-result of their work is always immensely satisfying, but they can be real arseholes along the way.

Tuesday 20th November 2012

I stopped going to the barber's about ten years ago. It was a forced retirement. I was devastated – I was in my early twenties and my hair had already stopped growing. The financial benefits didn't outweigh the stress it was causing, so I continued going for a lot longer than was strictly necessary. It was an embarrassing experience for both me and my barber, as we lightly danced around the elephant that wasn't only in the room, it was in the chair behind me, glancing up and waving every time I looked into the mirror. To be fair to the barber, he dragged it out as long as he could, snipping at imaginary bits of hair, brushing and coming bare bits of scalp and he did a fantastic job of angling the mirror at the end so that the light didn't bounce back and blind me.

What I hadn't realised at the time was that there was another benefit of not going to the barbers. I would never have to experience small-talk ever again. Why would an overweight man in his fifties, with a dodgy taste in shirts and a tan to rival David Dickinson's, want to know if I was going on holiday? My mum always told me never to talk to strange men, but not only am I talking to them, I'm giving them dates and times of my whereabouts.

The fact is that the barber feels as awkward as the customer when he's reeling off the classic one-liners such as "Going anywhere nice this year?" "How's life treating you?" and "What is it you do for a living?" but he feels compelled to do so, because he thinks that the dead space needs to be filled with talking. I honestly don't think it does. It's a noisy world out there and I actually think a lot of people would genuinely enjoy the experience of having their hair cut in silence.

Since I stopped going iPods and iPhones have taken off, so maybe these days kids just go in, pop one earphone out, tell the barber what they're after and then pop it back in. It would get a bit tricky around the ears with the various wires, but I'm sure the barbers would rather that than suffer the ridiculous charade that is small-talk.

If I were a barber I would sit the customer in the chair and as I am raising or lowering it, would simply say "Look, I'm not one for small-talk, you're probably uncomfortable telling strangers your intimate secrets and to be completely truthful, I'm not at all interested." Ok, it's not the friendliest opening gambit, but it's honest, and customers like honesty.

If I were a barber I would give my 'small-talk-free' customers the choice of silence or a quiz. A quiz is the perfect thing to get strangers talking, and most guys love a good quiz. You could have different subjects and difficulties based on the appearance of each customer. As soon as you saw a string vest you could be ready with the Jeremy Kyle quiz, and a pair of cords would see you scrabbling for the geography questions. I wouldn't suggest introducing this idea to beauty-salons though, as it is a fundamental requirement for the person asking the questions to be able to read.

This weekend I had to put up with a barrage of small-talk from a host of fifteen year-old girls. No, I wasn't at a One Direction gig – I had simply gone Christmas shopping. Now, while a fifty year-old man questioning a twenty-two year-old guy about his holiday plans might seem slightly sinister, a thirty-three year-old man telling a fifteen year-old girl that yes, he is looking forward to seeing Santa, is just wrong, no matter how you dress it up.

A fifteen year-old girl does not want to know about a thirty-three year-old man's plans for Christmas. She wants to know whether her mate Charlie got off with Jason who works at Clinton's.

I think all shop staff should be taught the basics in terms of customer service, ensuring that they are polite and friendly while never engaging in small-talk. Small-talk should never take place over a till. It is too short a transaction to give a proper response. I was genuinely tempted to go off on a long ramble about Aunty Julie not being able to get down this year because of her swollen ankles and the fact that Uncle Kevin might struggle because he hasn't had confirmation of his release date, but that would just have been cruel. I said what everyone else would say in the same situation, through gritted teeth. "Oh, I can't wait, it'll be lovely. It'll all be over soon though eh? Ha ha. Hee hee." etc, etc.

When I thought it was all over and I could finally escape the small-talk hell, I was met with a barrage of questions. It seems that the shops have already gone ahead with my earlier idea — they've gone down the quiz route!

"Would you like a bag with that?"

"Do you need help packing your bags?"

"Would you like the receipt in the bag?"

"Is this a present? Would you like it wrapped?"

"Have you thought about taking out a store-card?"

Questions, questions, questions.

Needless to say, I'll be doing the rest of my Christmas shopping online.

Bah humbug.

Wednesday 21st November 2012

My daughter loves to sing, and as we settled down to read a story before bed last night she launched into a rendition of "I love you", which is a sweet but irritating song sung by a huge purple dinosaur called Barney.

The lyrics are:

I love you.
You love me.
We're a happy family.
With a great bug hug and a kiss from me to you,
Won't you say you love me too?

As I said, sweet, but it is infuriatingly American, and by that I mean annoying. If there are any Americans reading, please don't take offence, I mean it in a very British way. By that I mean that I can't apologise enough! My daughter sang it with gusto, and it was only the second time around that I realised that she was getting the third line completely wrong. Instead of "We're a happy family", she was singing "We're a happy found a leaf".

I thought it was pretty cute and innocent, and I imagine it made perfect sense to her. To be fair, she often gets distracted, so I can imagine her thinking "We're a happy– oh look, I've found a leaf!" She perhaps just thought Barney was someone who was easily distracted.

She is three years old so she can be excused, but it did remind me of all the misheard lyrics I, and my friends, have been guilty of in the past. I remember being told off when I was young for singing "Now bring us some friggin' pudding" when singing "We wish you a Merry Christmas", and being exceptionally confused when corrected. Even now I don't really know what figgy pudding is, and only know of its existence through the song.

When I was about twelve Nirvana were pretty big and Smells Like Teen Spirit was a big anthem at the time, and a friend of mine misheard the lyric "Here we are now, entertain us", and instead used to sing "Here we are now, in containers".

The stupid thing is that we often don't question it; we just assume that the artist may have indulged in a few illegal remedies that day. With Kurt Cobain, that was almost a certainty.

My favourite misheard lyric was from a friend called Ben. He had just learned to drive and Bon Jovi's Crossroads album was constantly in the tape-deck. The song was Living on a Prayer, and the lyric was "It doesn't make a difference if we make it or not". He managed to hear it as "It doesn't make a difference if we're naked or not".

Now, most of the time, misheard lyrics don't make any sense, but this particular one kind of worked. The line before says that "we gotta hold on to what we got", and with the next few lines stating that they are "halfway there", that they will "give it a shot", and together they will "make it or not", it starts to paint a far steamier picture than the artist no doubt intended.

I seem to mishear lyrics all of the time, but not just in songs. Announcements always seem to say the strangest of things. I used to think "mind the gap" was "mind the bat". I actually thought the underground network was inundated with bats, and required regular announcements to warn us of their presence.

Even now, when the train I am currently sitting on announces that it will stop at

Headcorn, I hear "Bed Porn". This is incredibly stupid of me. Why?

Because I live in Headcorn.

Friday 23rd November 2012

As a commuter, I experience delays and cancellations on a regular basis. The railway network is huge, and there's a lot that can go wrong. After ten years of commuting, I've finally learned to accept this. In the last couple of years, however, I have noticed an increase in information and I'm not sure that I like it.

It was only a few years ago that the train would stop for no apparent reason. It would sit there for half an hour and then slowly hobble into platform number 76, and not a word would be said. If you dared to ask someone what had caused the delay, you would be met with nothing but a shrug and a blank stare. I'm not sure whether the new system of telling everybody everything is an order from the top, or whether the conductors are all just free-styling. Maybe they're all frustrated DJs.

I've counted more than fourteen announcements so far on my journey today. In my mind, that's about thirteen more than is actually necessary. The problem is that at every station we stop at, more people get on, so that is more people who need to be updated. Today

I have heard the following: "Apologies for the delay this morning, this is due to a cancelled train and congestion", which was swiftly followed by "Apologies for the earlier announcement which didn't fully explain the delay, and someone rightly pointed out that a cancelled train shouldn't cause congestion, but the train was cancelled due to an electrical fault and as it was stuck on the track, trains are having to be diverted around it, which is causing congestion."

We then had various versions of that message, together with confirmation of how late we were each time, which started off in five-minute increments and then increased to fifteen. We then had announcements as to how the trains behind us are getting on, followed by an announcement on how best to get to stations that this train isn't going to, owing to the cancellation of the earlier train. The final announcement told us how we could claim a refund on our journey as we were now over half an hour late.

I'm fully expecting the conductor to announce that there is a taxi outside in the name of Wilkins and that the next song is dedicated to Sheila and Brian, who after 40 years of marriage are retiring and moving to Spain.

Everyone around me seems quite relaxed about it and I know why that is; it's because we are on the way in to work. If this had happened on the way home from work, we would have a mutiny on our hands. There would be passengers relaying stories of how much they pay to be treated like cattle, there would be others detailing the exact dates and times of previous delays, and there would be lots and lots of shrugging, head-shaking and swearing under people's breath. All we have now is people frantically tapping on their Blackberries and laptops, and the odd muted sound of someone saying "Christine, can you let Paul know that I won't be able to make the 9:30; we'll have to reschedule".

I'm picking up two different vibes as I look around the train – one of frustration, and one of acceptance. This more or less correlates to those that are standing up and those that are seated. I've decided I'm going to give the lady in front of me a break and offer her my seat; she's most definitely in the frustrated camp. She's currently juggling two phones, a huge folder and a handbag that Mary Poppins would be proud of. She seems stressed, and is not only struggling to remain calm – she's struggling to stay on her feet.

Step forward the hero of the hour – the knight in shining armour!

Well that went down rather well. She very much appreciated me offering my seat and she is now able to spread her folder across her lap whilst carrying on with her phone call.

I would have liked to have ended the chapter there, as a proud hero, doing something selfless in someone's hour of need. But as I write this, one-handed, swaying about the train, struggling to piece together the last few sentences, she sits back, opens her handbag and begins to apply her make-up! Hour of need indeed.

Andy Leeks, what a bloody hero!

Tuesday 27th November 2012

As weekends go, the weekend just gone was pretty miserable. It rained the whole weekend, our daughter came down with a horrible cold, and I received an email from the gas and electricity company telling us our quarterly bills are due. In fact, the misery continues, as it is still raining, my daughter is still ill and I've still yet to pay those pesky bills. Oh and as if my misery weren't already complete, my train has just been cancelled and I'll now have to take a later train which will be twice as busy.

So here I am on a later train, squashed into a corner, soaked through and tired from a night of nursing my daughter, and I've got to find the inner strength to come up with something informative, thought-provoking or witty. The problem is, however, that I have just found out that the train I'm on does not stop where I need it to, meaning I have a choice between changing at the next stop and walking a long way in the rain. I've come to the conclusion that I can't be any more miserable than I currently am, so an extra walk in the rain can't hurt. Anyway, if I get off the train I might not be able to finish this chapter, which would be a plus-point for you, dear reader, believe me, but a definite failure on my part.

I'm aware that I'm moaning about trivial things and it is easy to forget that there are people with far greater worries out there. I know there are people who are starving, people living in poverty and people who are being exploited and abused. But those people don't have to put up with last-minute cancellations and constant delays, do they? I'm joking of course, but it is very easy to forget that our problems are tiny in comparison to others.

A few years ago Ashley Cole notoriously decided to include in his autobiography a chapter which detailed his anger at being offered only £55,000 a week instead of £60,000 while playing for Arsenal. The book was aimed at those who didn't earn that much in a year. That would be like me writing a cook-book for the starving.

It's a shorter chapter than usual today as I've had to write it with just one hand (my other one is trapped under either a person or a person's luggage, I'm not sure which, but either way, I'm pretty handicapped).

I'm hoping normal service will resume tomorrow, in terms of both trains and content.

Wednesday 28th November 2012

I love my neighbours. When I say that, I don't mean the Australian soap, I mean the people who live in the house attached to our house. We are extremely lucky to have such nice neighbours. I often hear of arguments and even fights between neighbours and it always seems to be down to car-parking or noise.

We are lucky enough to each have our own drive and, by living in an Edwardian house, we are also blessed with thick walls. Maybe that's it; maybe I've just stumbled across the magic ingredients for nationwide neighbour harmony. Never mind the 'Big Society', Mr Prime Minister; never mind 'Hug a Hoodie'. Let's tarmac everyone's drive and thicken everyone's walls. Imagine how nice it would be if everyone actually did 'love thy neighbour'. It would be like the 'Olympic Fever' all over again, only the feel-good factor would actually last longer than it took Jessica Ennis to complete her lap of honour.

If I'm honest, you could have the biggest drive in the world and the thickest possible walls, but if your neighbours are inconsiderate arseholes, there's really nothing you can do. They say to keep your friends close and your enemies closer, but being neighbours with your enemy is frankly ridiculous. Having to live next to a neighbour you hate would be like being forced to live with your ex, minus the knowledge of what they look like naked, hopefully. Although, saying that, a friend of mine used to regularly see his neighbour, a fifty-something widow, lying naked in the garden.

The reason we get on so well with our neighbours is that they are genuinely lovely people. They're kind, considerate, generous, funny, interesting and happy people, and not once have they been naked in the garden. We have only known them for seven months, but I already know that we have a friendship that will last years, if not a lifetime. It started off as a friendship out of circumstance; we decided to move and live out our lives three feet to one side of them, but very quickly it turned into a genuine friendship that had nothing to do with the proximity of our houses.

When you think about it, getting to know and then getting to like your neighbours is rather convenient. We have friends all over the place and often have to travel huge distances to meet up with them. If everyone became good friends with their neighbours, no-one would need to travel anywhere and we would solve global warming quicker than you can say "Can I borrow a cup of sugar, please?"

Yesterday, my wife found out that she needed to attend an important meeting at work and therefore couldn't take our daughter to nursery. Unfortunately I also had important engagements at work, so we were left in an awkward position. Step forward our lovely neighbours. Not only did they offer to drop our daughter off at nursery, they offered to look after her for a couple of hours first, even giving her breakfast, and ensuring we could both get to work in plenty of time.

As the famous line from the soap says, "Neighbours, everybody needs good neighbours!"

Friday 30th November 2012

I don't know what's happened to me this morning. Today is one of the busiest and most stressful days of the year for me. Today I have to finalise some very important figures, and these figures determine a lot of people's bonuses. It's a very sensitive time, especially this close to Christmas.

But instead of feeling stressed and apprehensive, I feel completely relaxed and content. This morning I was struck by the beauty of the planet that we live on, and it has left me feeling strangely humble and peaceful. No, I haven't gone mad and I haven't been drinking, I've just been noticing things this morning that I wouldn't normally notice.

When I first drew the curtains, I was greeted by a beautiful blackbird, sitting no more than three feet from my window. His feathers were plumped up, protecting him from the morning chill as the sun glistened and reflected off of his jet-black plumage. I was mesmerised by his beauty and needed the sound of the snoozed alarm-clock to bring me back from my trance.

As I trudged up the garden path and passed under the tree that housed my morning friend, I was met with a full moon and it stopped me in my tracks. The night before we had been blessed with a full moon that lit up the sky like a flare and I hadn't expected to see it again so soon. It was on the opposite side of the sky to the night before, and its silvery glow had been replaced by a wispy, cloud-like white. It was elegant and beautiful, silent and stunning.

As I sit here now, on the train, describing the sights which have humbled me, I can see vast, rolling hills covered in a blanket of white frost. There is smoke rising from the chimneys of distant cottages and church towers peeping into view, partially hidden by the hills before them. The last of the autumn leaves are floating gently to the ground as the trails from long-gone planes leave a lattice of white stripes overhead.

As I lose myself in the beauty which sits outside my window, I am interrupted by a loud crackle, followed by an announcement. "Ladies and gentlemen, we are now approaching London Bridge; please remember to take all of your belongings with you."

It's on days like these that I wish the conductors would go off-piste, forget about lost property and bomb-threats and do what pilots do so well. Describe the beauty sitting outside the window.

"Ladies and gentlemen, it's 7:54 am, we should be arriving into London by 8:40. If you look outside the window to your left you will see the beautiful parish church of Smarden. The current church was built between 1325 and 1350 of local Kentish ragstone and Bethersden marble quarried at nearby Tuesnoad. Now if you look to your right......"

Monday 3rd December 2012

Today marks twenty years since the first text message was sent and received. I suppose that is an important point – the fact that it was also actually received. I imagine that anyone could claim to have sent the first text. There could have been thousands of texts sent over the last hundred years or so, but they just weren't being received.

"Shit, just heard that J F K got shot!"

"Who would have thought it, a woman for a Prime Minister?!"

"Apparently there's gonna be a big storm tomorrow. Don't worry though – Michael Fish said it will all be alright, lol"

"Just heard that some guy called Hitler has invaded Poland"

"OMG, the Titanic has sunk"

The person who actually sent the first text was a guy called Neil Papworth, a 22 year-old telecom engineer who worked for a company developing text communication on behalf of Vodafone. He sent it to one of the directors, who was at a Christmas party, and the message simply read "Merry Christmas". That's a lovely story and a great quiz question, but surely they should have thought of something better than that.

This was a groundbreaking moment and they surely would have known that at the time. Why didn't he send something like:

"If this works, I want a pay rise"

Or

"Just think before you have that next glass of red, we're meeting Bob from Vodafone tomorrow"

Or

"Can you please not leave me on the dressing table tonight? I deserve to be on your bedside table, with your glasses and your crossword"?

I'm not a massive fan of text messaging. The only time I find it acceptable is when asking and answering simple questions.

"What time will you be home?"

"8pm"

As soon as it goes beyond this simple function, I find it infuriating to use. The problem with the written word, and the written word in the form of mobile texting in particular, is that it's often misunderstood and taken out of context. A polite request can suddenly seem rude, or a simple question can come across as an invasion of privacy. I spend so long re-writing texts so they cannot be misunderstood, that it's always quicker to call. The problem for me is that I also hate calling people. I'm always worried that I'm disturbing them, so I tend not to bother to text or phone anyone if I can help it.

I know it's old fashioned, but I actually like the process of sending and receiving letters. Ok, it's an incredibly slow and expensive way of communicating, but people always seem genuinely pleased to receive a letter. Can you imagine receiving a personal letter through the door and thinking "Oh, it's him again, what does he want this time?"

(Famous people with stalkers don't have to answer that last question.)

You can be completely honest in a letter and you will never cause any upset. The fact that someone has taken the time to write something and physically post it means they will almost always be let off the hook. Every now and then there are situations where you need to be honest. These situations tend to manifest themselves as your best friend asking your opinion on his latest haircut, or deciding to go through that phase of thinking that dungarees are cool. A letter is genuinely the only way of dealing with this type of awkward situation. I've lost count of the letters I have sent to ex-girlfriends saying "Yes your arse does look fat in that", or "It wasn't you, it was me".

It was also reported today that, for the first time, texts are actually in decline. I was initially optimistic, thinking that letters might be making a comeback, but I'm disappointed to report that texts are just being replaced by social networking sites and free messaging apps.

So unfortunately, we will have to go on living in a world where dodgy haircuts are the norm, where dungarees are still being purchased by adults, and where arses continue to look fat in things.

Tuesday 4th December 2012

I'm writing this while standing up today. I've never minded standing up while commuting, even though my journey takes well over an hour. My theory is that I sit down all day, so standing up for an hour isn't exactly a hardship. There are people who have to stand all day in order to do their job, so it's they who deserve a seat.

I would actually be happy if the train companies announced that they were going to introduce priority passes for those who work in upright professions. In fact, thinking about it, wouldn't it make it simpler if you were issued a pass based on your personal circumstances? There should be a priority sit-down pass for anyone who works in an upright profession, anyone with a disability, anyone over sixty and anyone who is pregnant. Everyone else is issued with a non-priority pass, meaning they have to give up their seat once someone with a priority pass asks to sit down.

I would actually go one stage further and introduce three differently coloured passes – a green one for those who qualify to sit down at any time, an orange one for those who don't qualify, and a red one for those who actively opt out of sitting down altogether and elect to stand up. Those going for a red pass would maybe even qualify for some kind of discount.

I'm sure this system would create harmony amongst travellers as there would be less squabbling for seats, and it would mean those in the upright professions can get more rest and therefore do a better job. I can't see many negatives here. The only real negative is the one I'm experiencing right now, in that I have to type this with one hand.

The reason I'm currently standing is that I gave up my seat to a young mother and child. As I've mentioned before, I sit by the toilets, but it is also the area for wheelchairs and pushchairs. I have actually given up my seat for this same lady a number of times, and she is always very appreciative. It seems to be Tuesdays and Fridays that she has the child with her, and I am effectively responsible for keeping her seat warm.

You may ask why I continue to sit in the seat, knowing full well that I will end up having to move, but I do it for a very good reason. If I didn't give up my seat it is highly likely that she and her young daughter would have to stand for the whole journey. It is amazing how many young, male professionals seem to get a little bit sleepy, or suddenly find an article about coastal erosion absolutely fascinating as soon as she steps on board.

I've often given up my seat to people who wouldn't normally come under the 'Priority' category. I genuinely don't care whether I sit down or not, so when I see someone upset at having to stand, I will invariably offer my seat. It doesn't matter whether they are old, female, pregnant, or none of the above; if they would prefer to sit down and I'm not bothered, then I'll offer them my seat.

It's a very simple form of charity, and it has made me realise that I don't do enough in that respect. When I look around my house there is plenty of stuff I no longer want or need, and there are people less fortunate than me who could either use it, or use the money raised from it. With Christmas coming up, there is no better time to clear out the spare room and take a trip down to the charity-shop.

When I started writing this book, I saw it as an opportunity to be creative and share my view on the world around me, but it's turning into more of a voyage of self-discovery and enlightenment. Ok, maybe that's going a bit far, but I'm definitely going to clear out all the crap in the spare room, so I've got this book to thank for that!

Wednesday 5th December 2012

The train is delayed again this morning, but there are no broken-down trains, no staff shortages, no engineering works and no-one has committed suicide. Today we have delays because of "poor rail conditions".

Have the rails caught an illness? Have they suddenly deteriorated overnight? No. We have poor rail conditions because approximately twenty minutes ago we had a light flurry of snowfall, which lasted about three minutes.

I don't like to moan about the trains because in general, I think we enjoy a good service, but on days like today I am left scratching my head. There can't be more than a millimetre of snow on the tracks at the present time – how can this delay a five thousand-tonne train?

Do trains experience delays in the snow because the tracks are slippery? If that's the case then surely a simple fix would be to heat the rails or introduce some sort of a modification to the wheels where a button can be pressed and extra grip can be generated. I'm assuming the reason we don't have these features available to us is the cost. I get a cold sweat every time I receive a gas bill for my house, so I would hate to see what the bill would be to heat a whole network of rails. Cars have traction control and ABS, though; surely trains can have that too?

Apparently it's not always down to the simple fact that the rails get a bit slippery, there are a whole number of contributing factors. Points start to freeze up, equipment starts to fail and train staff find it difficult to get to work. Add all of this to "poor rail conditions" and you start to get a knock-on effect where delays turn into cancellations, and cancellations mean sweary commuters.

I have an idea to combat the weather issues. There will never be any problems with snow and there will never be any issues with leaves on the track. How about, now I know this might sound crazy, but how about we build a network of rails… underground?

We could call it the 'Underground', and as all of the equipment would be underground, nothing would break or fail, and there would be no issues with staff getting to work, meaning there would never be any delays and everyone would be happy with the service.

Next week, I'll be suggesting an extra lane to completely eradicate congestion on the M25, and a coalition government to finally sort out the political malaise.

Friday 7th December 2012

Train etiquette is very much like bus or toilet etiquette. There is an unspoken rule that everyone adheres to. You must head for the areas that are sparsely populated. This means that once on a bus or train, you must look for empty seats in clusters of two and men in a public toilet should always look for a cluster of three, as it guarantees a space either side. This unspoken rule is completely instinctive. It doesn't have to be taught or handed down generation after generation, it is just good old human nature.

Would I rather sit next to the guy reading Carp of the Week and with breakfast down his chin or would I rather just sit on my own. Would I rather stand within four inches of another mans penis while emptying my bladder, or would I rather just pee in peace. (I was nervous when deciding on the distance to go with in that last sentence, using inches and penis in the same sentence is always tricky. I went for four inches because no-one likes a show off)

On busy days of course, this theory goes out of the window and it is every man, woman and child for themselves. This is accepted and this is fine. So long as you follow the basic principles up until the point where there are more people than clusters of two's and three's then you won't be labelled a weirdo.

The weirdo got onto the train about ten minutes ago.

I'm staring at him now.

He seems quite normal really; his hair is neat and tidy, he looks presentable, he's not reading Carp of the Week and there are no visible signs of his breakfast. Why then, when there are many clusters of empty seats, has he sat next to someone. Initially, I thought he knew the other person, but if they know each other, they clearly don't like each other because they are not talking. Stranger still, he didn't just slide in next to him, he had to ask him to move so he could sit down by the window.

Hang on, they're talking, maybe they do know each other after all.

Ok, I have an update.

After an awkward silence and a fair bit of huffing and puffing from the rightly disgruntled passenger, our weirdo has explained that he likes to sit by the window, facing forward and this was the only seat that was free that fitted that description. He then went on to say that he liked to see where he was going. What, just in case the driver takes a wrong turn and takes us to Margate for the day? What is he expecting to see today that he didn't see yesterday? I would absolutely love to kick off my shoes and put my feet up while travelling, but I don't because firstly, I am considerate to the other passengers and secondly I am not a weirdo.

Please, everyone reading; don't be a weirdo and just follow the simple rules of train etiquette.

Thank you

Monday 10th December 2012

Real or fake, that seems to be the main debate at the moment. Fake ones look great and they never droop, but they just don't feel the same, do they?

I'm talking about Christmas trees of course and this weekend saw us buying our annual 8 foot tree before cutting it down to six, so that it fits. Real Christmas trees tend to get a bad press. Like naughty teenagers they are often charged with being temperamental and messy. Well, like teenagers, if you get the right one, they can be totally worth the effort. Ok, our Christmas trees have never tidied up after themselves or made us a cup of tea after a hard day, but they do tend to stay fairly mess free and they always produce a pleasant smell; far nicer than the dusty aroma that I associate with a fake one.

People often say "It's just such an effort! Going out, choosing one, bringing it back, dragging it through the house, getting pine needles everywhere....." That sounds a lovely day out compared to the rigmarole involved with setting up our old fake tree. My Mum and Dad have never got around to installing a proper loft ladder. Not the crime of the century you might think, but they never got around to buying more than a four foot step ladder either. The loft hatch in my Mum and Dads house hovers dangerously over the stairs and only a highly trained acrobat from the Moscow State Circus would attempt an entry via the step ladder. Every year however, my Dad would come back from the pub and announce that it was time for the tree to come down. This happened every year until my brother was old enough / tall enough to take over and he had two main advantages over my Dad in that he was 20 years younger in age and 20 units lighter in alcohol.

On a slight digression, while talking about my Dad insisting on doing things while under the influence, I remember one year where my Mum had gone Christmas food shopping. She had gone out in the morning and come back late in the afternoon and the car was full of festive food. Dad had been to the pub to meet a few old friends and had consumed, shall we say "A festive few."

My Mum had spent ages trying to rearrange our freezer to fit in all of the frozen food, but it wasn't any good, it just wasn't fitting in. It was one of those combination fridge/freezers that stood about six foot tall, with the freezer compartment at the bottom and the fridge on top. She had noticed that the freezer was thick with ice and if it could be defrosted, she would be able to fit in all of the food.

Step forward my dad, with a hammer in one hand and a pallet knife in the other. The reason that he had a hammer just lying around was simple. Dad always put all of the decorations up with a hammer. I am certain that we were the only family that had no use for blue tac at Christmas. The tree was hammered together with a mallet and everything else from lights to stockings were attached to the wall with a hammer and nail.

We heard a combination of banging and swearing for just under an hour before it all went quiet. After a few minutes, we decided to go and check to see if everything was ok and what we witnessed was like a scene from a Laurel and Hardy movie. My Dad was sitting on the floor holding his head, completely dazed, while our dog was running around the kitchen gobbling up a floor full of pickled onions.

It didn't need Colombo to work out that while Dad was getting to work with the bottom compartment of the freezer, the catering sized jar of pickled onions on top of the fridge/freezer was slowly making it's way towards his head. The thought of my Dad being nursed by my Mum; who was holding up a combination of fingers while the dog gagged in the background still makes me laugh today.

So our Christmas tree is up and the decorations are in place and I haven't once had to use any carpentry tools or acrobatics. I just need to make sure that I defrost the freezer before the food shopping arrives.

Tuesday 11th December 2012

Today is the last chapter of the book. It marks an interesting and emotional three months where I have blathered on about a variety of things, such as introducing a 22nd birthday, lying when returning unwanted gifts, introducing an interactive news show, moving Halloween to June, banning mobility carts, why I can't complain, why I hate small talk and why my Dad uses a hammer to put up Christmas Decorations.

It hasn't all been a load of rambling nonsense, there have been times of sadness, where I had to say goodbye to my dear old Gramps; there have been times of reflection, where I decided I needed to put other people first and there have been times of realisation; where I saw the beauty of the world around me and was humbled by it's elegance and simplicity. There are also times where I moaned about my zits and explained why I couldn't poo in public, so let's not pretend that these are the works of Chaucer.

As it is the end of the book, it is the perfect time to tie up a few of the loose ends. Early on in the book, I mentioned that I would start bringing my own coffee to work in a flask. I decided that it would be a real money saver, possibly saving as much as £448.64 in a year. This idea was fantastic in principle, but I quickly learned that it is a false economy. My workings only accounted for one flask. The problem is that I keep leaving them on the train, meaning I have to keep buying new flasks. I'm on the 5th or 6th one since I started the book, so I reckon I'm probably just about even.

On the 5th of November I challenged myself to lose twenty pounds in just under six weeks. This was all very well at the time, but what I hadn't factored in was that effectively, the Christmas season starts on the 1st of December and ever since then, I have been gorging on mince pies and chocolates. I'm happy to announce that I am currently wearing my old work trousers and I have lost around a stone in weight, but I didn't manage to lose the twenty pounds I had hoped.

Oh and maybe I am being too honest here, but I never did manage to get down the charity shop, but I promise I will do before Christmas.

So that is it, a strange three months that started with an argument on Facebook and ended with me listing my many failings.

I will continue to write while I commute and I hope to release Part Two towards the end of March 2013. If you are interested in receiving updates or just wish to drop me a line, you can do so at astheyslept@yahoo.co.uk

You can also keep up to date with the book on Facebook, after all, that's where it all started. If you liked the book, please feel free to "like" and "share" the page. If you didn't I'm sad to say that Facebook has yet to come up with a "dislike" button, so the best I can suggest is for you to send me an offensive email of some sort.

You can find the Facebook page by going to

www.facebook.com/astheyslept

Special Thanks

Emma and Charlotte – For your constant support and happy smiles.

Euan Davidson – For being a truly great editor and answering all of my stupid questions.

Steve Lawson – For providing the graphic design and expertise required to make this book look as good as it does.

Dean Mason – For providing the inspiration for the book and an honest if not altogether positive foreword for the book

My mum and dad – Everyone thanks their mum and dad don't they?

Printed in Great Britain
by Amazon.co.uk, Ltd.,
Marston Gate.